For
Christopher Simpson
Thank you for all you have
done for the School of Medicine.
With best wishes of the author—

Walter B. Edgar
19 August 93

South Carolina
in the Modern Age

South Carolina

in the Modern Age

Walter B. Edgar

University of South Carolina Press

Published in Columbia, South Carolina,
by the University of South Carolina Press

Printed in Canada

Library of Congress Cataloging-in-Publication Data

Edgar, Walter B., 1943–
South Carolina in the Modern Age/Walter B. Edgar.
p. cm.
Includes bibliographical references and index.
ISBN 0-87249-830-1 (hard cover : acid free). — ISBN 0-87249-831-X (pbk. : acid free)
1. South Carolina—History—1865– I. Title.
F274.E34 1992
975.7'04—dc20 92-9357

for
Eliza and Amelia

CONTENTS

ILLUSTRATIONS

PREFACE

South Carolina is one of the most fascinating, yet most often misunderstood, states in the Union. Surveys taken outside the South reveal that "average Americans" usually confuse the Palmetto State with its neighbor to the north. This lack of identity is the result of history and South Carolina's role in it.

Prior to 1860, what South Carolina and her leaders did was important on both sides of the Atlantic. During the colonial period, South Carolina was the wealthiest mainland British colony—one of the crown jewels of the empire. Between the American Revolution and the outbreak of the Civil War, how the state and its leaders reacted to issues was of concern to politicians in Washington.

Then the events of 1860-61 changed matters. South Carolina led the South out of the Union and into war, a war that was not kind to either the state or the region. Because of its role in the breakup of the Union, the state paid a price—especially in the history books. Because of the war, South Carolina lost a generation of young white men and virtually all of its capital wealth. It recovered from the former, but it has yet to recover from the latter.

With relatively little political clout and a poverty-stricken population, South Carolina disappeared from the national scene. It appeared as if the state had sunk into a lethargy which it did not shake off until after World War II. In South Carolina between 1891 and 1991, appearances were truly deceiving. Within its borders changes were taking place that would enable the state to jump from the eighteenth century to the twentieth in only a matter of years.[1]

Kelly Miller, a sociologist and historian, in 1925 described his native state in this fashion: "South Carolina is the stormy petrel of the Union. She arouses the nation's wrath and rides upon the storm. There is not a dull period in her history."[2] Benjamin Brawley, a contemporary of Miller, was even more emphatic when he discussed the role of the Palmetto State: "The little triangle on the map known as South Carolina represents a portion of our country whose influence has been incalculable."[3]

This book examines the third century of South Carolina history from the rise of the populist Ben Tillman with his political and agricultural agendas of the 1890s to the Sun Belt development of the 1990s. It is divided into four essays, each of which examines a quarter century. The chronological breakdown has been determined as much by outside events as by those within South Carolina. The first essay deals with the time period from the triumph of Pitchfork Ben Tillman to the reelection of President Woodrow Wilson; the second from Wilson to the country's entry into World War II; the third from the war to the unopposed reelection of Governor Robert E. McNair; and the fourth from McNair, a "New South Governor," to the present. Originally, I had planned to end the book in 1990, but the events of 1990-91 seemed to me to provide a more fitting conclusion.

As someone who has taught South Carolina history at the state's flagship university since the mid 1970s, I have long felt that there was a need for a new contemporary history of the state. Natives as well as newcomers know little about twentieth-century Carolina and the people and forces that shaped it.

The last contemporary history of the state was Ernest M. Lander's *A History of South Carolina, 1865-1960.* A great deal has transpired in the three decades since the first year of the observance of the Confederate War Centennial.[4] If anyone could have described the South Carolina of 1991 to Carolinians of 1960, they would have had him or her committed to Bull Street.[5] The past thirty years have seen changes in South Carolina that would have been unthinkable then. There was a need to chronicle these changes and reinterpret earlier events in the light of recent scholarship and newly discovered primary material.

ACKNOWLEDGMENTS

Slightly different versions of these essays first appeared in *The State* newspaper as part of its centennial observances. I am grateful to *The State* and its staff for its support and cooperation, especially Ben Morris, Tom McLean, and Bill Starr. They allowed me the freedom to research and tell the state's story as I found it.

Although I spent a productive sabbatical year (1989-90) completing these essays, they are the products of more than a quarter century of a journey through the records of the South Caroliniana Library, the South Carolina Historical Society, and the South Carolina Department of Archives and History.

In the third essay I noted that as late as 1966 politics in South Carolina were still the politics of "friends and neighbors." That may have changed, but in this state, historical research is more than merely checking records. It is also learning from colleagues who also are friends and neighbors—individuals such as Thorne Compton, Edward Cox, Don Fowler, Gus Graydon, Ben Greer, Dan Hollis, Tom Johnson, Lewis Jones, Chas Joyner, Chuck Kovacik, George Rogers, Alex Moore, Ed Smith, Jack Sproat, Allen Stokes, and Bill Workman.

One of the pleasures of directing the Institute for Southern Studies is the chance to interact with other scholars interested in South Carolina: Barbara Bellows, John Byars, Kathy Cann, Marvin Cann, David Carlton, Peter Coclanis, Veronica Davis-Gerald, Lacy Ford, John McCardell, Bob Simpson, Lewis Suggs, George Terry, and Barbara Woods.

As part of *The State*'s centennial publications, I worked closely with four colleagues from across the state: John Edmunds of the University of South Carolina-Spartanburg, Blease Graham of the University of South Carolina-Columbia, A. V. Huff, Jr., of Furman University, and Amy McCandless of the College of Charleston. During the course of the project, we came to share a common concern for the future of our state as we chronicled its past.

Doing research in South Carolina is made easier by the people who staff the various collections: Alexia Helsley and the

Search Room staff at the South Carolina Department of Archives and History, Mark Wetherington and his staff at the South Carolina Historical Society, Allen Stokes and the entire staff of the South Caroliniana Library, and Dargan Richards of *The State's* reference collection. Charles Gay and Lewis Ziegler did photography for this book. I am especially grateful to the South Carolina Historical Society, the South Carolina State Museum, the South Caroliniana Library, *The State*, and various individuals for permission to use photographs from their collections.

At the Institute for Southern Studies, Tibby Dozier and Nancy Ashmore Cooper kept the office running smoothly while I was on sabbatical. They and Suzanne Linder helped with the necessary chores of completing the manuscript for publication.

The University of South Carolina granted me sabbatical leave to complete this project. In this, as in other endeavors, Dean Carol McGinnis Kay of the College of Humanities and Social Sciences has been very supportive.

Writing local history also has its drawbacks. Normally one takes a sabbatical leave away from one's home institution and hides out in a faraway place. Given the subject at hand and the local resources, leaving town didn't make much sense. Staying away from the office did make good sense and was possible only because my wife Betty and our daughters Eliza and Amelia made sure that I could work undisturbed at home.

Betty not only saw to it that I could work at home, but also worked with me as the manuscript took shape. In August 1991 we celebrated our twenty-fifth wedding anniversary. Together we have lived through one-fourth of the history recorded here.

This book, describing how late-twentieth-century South Carolina came to be, is dedicated to my daughters Eliza and Amelia. They will make their homes in this new South Carolina, a South Carolina strikingly different from the one I first encountered as a new graduate student at the University of South Carolina in September 1965.

South Carolina
in the Modern Age

Chapter 1

A POLITICAL BULLRING, 1891–1916

Politics since the early colonial days have been the South Carolina bull ring. The passions profitlessly expended in it if turned into other energies might have produced a great literature or a triumphant industrial civilization.

—David Duncan Wallace,
History of South Carolina (1934)

Professor Wallace's description of the role politics have played in South Carolina history was certainly appropriate for the years between 1891 and 1916. Few periods in the state's history have seen as much political activity.

Politics were entertainment in turn-of-the-century South Carolina. In 1909 Governor Martin J. Ansel spoke in Georgetown. *Courtesy South Caroliniana Library.*

Facing a changing world, a world in which their state was considered less important than most backwater European colonies, white South Carolinians struggled among themselves for control over their changing society. Agriculture was depressed. Textile mills appeared all across the Piedmont, creating a new business-oriented elite and a white working class. Railroads turned country crossroads into market centers which, in turn, gave rise to the growth of a solid middle class.

These simultaneous alterations in South Carolina's economic and social fabrics led to political instability. The old, pre–Civil War elite which had reestablished its control over the state in 1877 was out of touch and incapable of dealing with the situation. Farmers, mill workers, and middle-class reformers saw opportunities for their respective causes and for a quarter century vied for control of state and local governments.

Some Background: The United States in 1890

In 1890, across the country, there was discontent with governmental and economic institutions. Since 1887, farmers in the South and the West had battled drought, low prices, and debts. There was more labor unrest in 1890 than in any other year in the century, although the violent Homestead and Pullman strikes were still a few years off.

The Panic of 1893 added to the nation's economic woes. By the end of the year four million American workers were jobless. In an attempt to stabilize the economy, President Grover Cleveland asked J. P. Morgan to market government bonds and Congress to repeal the Sherman Silver Purchase Act.

Farmers felt betrayed. The President had sold out to "Wall Street," which they considered the root of all that was wrong with American society. They were incensed by reports in the popular press of new millionaires' conspicuous consumption. While tens of thousands of hard working men and women were losing their farms to banks, nouveaux riches built multi-million-dollar "summer cottages" at Newport. Something was wrong. Thomas Jefferson's yeoman farmer no longer seemed to matter to the nation's political parties. In frustration, voters in the West turned in 1892 to the People's Party.

Four years later, southern and western farmers seized control of the Democratic Party, denounced Cleveland, and coopted the Populists' revolutionary platform—all to no avail. Bryan was defeated, and the political victory of business and industry over agriculture did little to solve the country's problems. Reform-minded citizens began to work together to improve their communities. Eventually their determined efforts, fueled by the venal excesses of the Gilded Age, would lead to the Progressive Era and major national reforms.

South Carolina in 1890

As South Carolina entered the last decade of the nineteenth century, its politics were just as unsettled as those of the rest of the nation and the reasons for the state's political unrest were similar to those elsewhere.

Observers described the state and its people in less than flattering terms. Some of the negative comments came from northerners still getting in their licks for the state's role in the secession crisis; however, among the chief critics of the "state of the state" were some of its native sons.[1] They denounced the general lethargy that was a way of life for many South Carolinians.

Poverty and ignorance were cited as causes of the state's woes, but were they the cause or were they the effect? One of the nation's wealthiest states in 1860, South Carolina ranked near the bottom in per capita income in 1890.[2] Poverty and debt were very real. In the late 1880s Carolinians forfeited more than one million acres of land for nonpayment of taxes.[3] Debt was a crushing burden to those who tilled the soil. In any given year, 30 to 60 percent of the cotton crop was obligated for debt payments prior to harvest.[4]

In a vain attempt to increase their incomes, farmers planted more cotton. Subsistence farming was abandoned. Cotton production was twice what it had been in 1860, but increased cotton production across the South caused prices to plummet.[5] Railroad rates were outrageous and designed to funnel South Carolina produce directly to northern markets rather than through Charleston. For example, it cost $0.46 to ship a bale of cotton from Abbeville to New York City, but $1.50 to ship one from Abbeville to Charleston.[6]

Illiteracy was a scandal. And so was public health—or the lack thereof. With 45 percent of the population totally illiterate, it should be no surprise that the state's poor suffered from a variety of diseases.[7] The young men of South Carolina were in such poor physical condition that rejection rates for white volunteers during the Spanish-American War would run as high as 44 percent in some upcountry counties.[8] The condition of the state mirrored that of many of her people. South Carolina was in wretched shape economically. The Civil War was blamed for

By the 1890s, South Carolinians produced three times as much cotton as they had in 1860. Georgetown's docks were a busy place during the late fall. *Courtesy South Caroliniana Library.*

The unfinished State House, "a roofed over barn," symbolized the poverty into which South Carolina had fallen after the Civil War. *Courtesy South Caroliniana Library.*

the state's difficulties, but, in reality, the war simply had exacerbated problems that had existed since the 1820s.[9]

State government did little to assist the farmers. In fact, state government did very little at all. The inaction of those in office was due, in no small part, to their reaction to the excesses of the Reconstruction regime they had overthrown in 1877.[10] To observers this lethargy (a few cruel ones called it atrophy) permeated South Carolina from top to bottom. Appearances, however, can be deceiving.

The state was on the verge of entering a turbulent quarter century (1891–1916) in which traditional beliefs and institutions would be challenged, altered, and, in some cases, discarded. South Carolina's government, economy, and society would all undergo fundamental changes. The South Carolina that emerged from these twenty-five years of turmoil would survive intact into the 1960s.

Those in power, the old pre–Civil War elite, were out of touch with the general population. To their friends, they were "the Redeemers," the men who had saved South Carolina from the horrors of black and Republican rule. To their enemies, they were "the Bourbons," akin to the restored monarchists of nineteenth-century France who had forgotten what had caused their downfall and repeated their mistakes.

Regardless of the labels, they were, for the most part, older men who did not understand the problems facing the state. For them, it was enough to campaign as a war hero of '65 or a Red Shirt of '76.[11]

Although Tillman denounced the state's old guard politicians (most of whom were Confederate veterans), individual Confederate veterans were still treated as heroes. In May 1910 veterans posed in front of the State House. ***Courtesy South Caroliniana Library.***

To the discontented farmers, struggling to hang onto their debt-ridden farms, past glories didn't help feed or clothe their families. Collapsing farm prices, worn-out soils, exorbitant credit rates (as high as 100% in some counties), and the Bourbons' policy of racial moderation led to considerable discontent among rural whites. What the disgruntled farmers needed was a spokesman.[12]

The Rise of Ben Tillman

In 1885, after a fiery speech in Bennettsville before a joint meeting of the state Grange and the South Carolina Agricultural and Mechanical Society, the farmers found their leader: Benjamin Ryan Tillman of Edgefield County. Tillman electrified his audience by attacking the state's "do nothing" leaders; however, he offered some positive recommendations as well. Chief among his proposals was the creation of a separate agricultural college for the sons of "real farmers." The proposal for an agricultural college became the highest priority of the Farmers' Association, a new group formed specifically to promote Tillman's ideas. Very quickly the nonpartisan association became a vehicle for Tillman's political ambitions.

The idea for another state-supported school was opposed vigorously by friends of the Citadel, the University of South Carolina, and South Carolina's numerous denominational schools. It appeared that the proposal would get nowhere, but then Thomas G. Clemson died and willed his upcountry estate and $80,000 to the state of South Carolina for the purpose of establishing an agricultural college. The issue was joined. After furious debate, the General Assembly in 1889 voted to accept Clemson's gift. USC's College of Agriculture was closed and Morrill Act funds were given to the new institution. Four years later Clemson College admitted its first students.

The Clemson legacy opened the political doors for Ben Tillman. Hard on the heels of the bitter fight for an agricultural college, he maneuvered the Farmers' Association into nominating a slate of candidates for statewide office prior to the Democratic Party Convention.[13]

To no one's surprise, the Farmers' Association nominated Tillman for governor. In a vigorous statewide campaign, he made effective use of innuendoes, half-truths, and bald-faced lies to destroy whatever following the Bourbons still might have among the electorate. He openly sneered at the "broken down aristocrats" who viewed the world "through ante-bellum spectacles" and "marched backwards when they marched at all."[14]

Ben Tillman established Winthrop College in Rock Hill primarily to train teachers. Field hockey was a popular sport at the all-girl school. ***Courtesy South Caroliniana Library.***

His opponents, now calling themselves "Conservatives," underestimated Tillman. They dismissed him as a "ranting country cracker." They were totally unprepared for the vicious campaign of 1890. Old Confederate heroes, even the venerated Wade Hampton, were hooted down at stump meetings.[15]

The voters seemed to care little for the facts or for real debate. It did not matter that Tillman at times contradicted himself on issues. They preferred hearing him ridicule "the greedy old city of Charleston" and its "dude factory," the Citadel, or "the seedbed of the aristocracy," the University of South Carolina. He played up class prejudices every chance he got. Comments such as "I am simply a clod-hopper like you are" brought wildly cheering audiences to their feet.[16]

Tillman triumphed at the Democratic Convention. His opponents bolted and openly appealed to the state's remaining black voters. All they did was play into Tillman's hands. He scored a smashing victory at the polls, and for the next decade his word was law in South Carolina.

One of the enduring results of Tillman's election was the creation of a newspaper in the state capital that would expose "the tyrant" for what he was. Thus, *The State* was born. The Conservatives who backed the paper persuaded a former Charleston *News and Courier* reporter, N. G. Gonzales, to become its editor.[17] Tillman soon discovered that he had a determined adversary in *The State.*

In office Tillman was ruthless in dealing with his foes. He ordered his followers to vote against the reelection of Senator Wade Hampton, and the old war hero was defeated. With commanding majorities in both houses of the General Assembly after 1892, he did what he wanted.[18] The voters be damned.

The Dispensary, a state liquor monopoly, was one of the most blatant examples of Tillman's dictatorial nature. In a referendum the state's voters had overwhelmingly supported prohibition. In 1892 a prohibition bill was before the General Assembly, but the governor had it altered to create the Dispensary.[19] It quickly became a source of controversy and corruption. The Dispensary was very unpopular in Charleston, Columbia, and the towns of the Pee Dee region. In Darlington, Dispensary constables roughed up some local citizens. When

The Dispensary, a state liquor monopoly, was one of Governor Tillman's most controversial projects. The Dispensary imported whiskey in bulk which was then bottled in this Columbia plant. ***Courtesy South Caroliniana Library.***

the town's police chief tried to arrest the constables, one of them fired into a crowd, killing a bystander and touching off a riot.

Fueled by sensational stories in *The State*, the Greenville *News*, and the Charleston *News and Courier*, South Carolina teetered on the brink of civil disorder. Governor Tillman declared Darlington and Florence counties to be in a state of insurrection. He called up militia companies to quell the rioting, but the militia in Charleston, Columbia, Manning, and Sumter refused to report for duty. There was fear of disorder in Columbia, but that was quelled by the appearance of militia companies from Edgefield and Newberry. They were posted at the State House, the Dispensary warehouse, and the Governor's Mansion. Within a week, the "Dispensary War" was over, but it had served as an indication of the serious divisions within South Carolina's body politic.

In 1894 Tillman was elected to the U.S. Senate. During his first few years in Washington, he kept a tight rein on his followers back home.

Legalizing Jim Crow

The 1890 census returns had not brought any comfort to white South Carolinians. In twenty-nine of the state's thirty-six counties, blacks were a majority of the population. In the state as a whole, whites were more of a minority (40.1 percent) than they had been in 1860 (41.1 percent).[20]

The presence of the black majority had taken on a new meaning in 1865 when blacks were freed and given the right to vote. During Reconstruction blacks participated actively in politics. Beginning in the 1870s, intimidation and violence were used to keep them from the polls.

In lowcountry counties, overwhelming black majorities resulted in continued black participation in politics through the 1880s. In Georgetown County, the "Fusion Plan" of 1880 divided offices between black Republicans and white Democrats. In Beaufort, most officeholders were black. The so-called "Black Congressional District," stretching from Beaufort to lower Richland County, had a black congressman until 1896.[21] Although there were black Democrats, the vast majority of black Carolinians were Republicans. In statewide elections after 1876, fewer and fewer cast their ballots.

One of Tillman's pieces of unfinished business was to deal with the state's remaining black voters.

Branchville in Orangeburg County was typical of many rural communities. ***Courtesy South Caroliniana Library.***

The Conservatives' open appeal for black votes in 1890 had shocked most white Carolinians. They supported Tillman's view that blacks should not hold the balance of power between competing white factions.[22] In order to eliminate black voters, Tillman opted for rewriting the state's constitution. The statewide referendum on calling a constitutional convention passed by fewer than a thousand votes. Generally upcountry voters favored calling the convention and lowcountry voters did not.

During the debates in the convention, an unusual grouping of Conservative, black, and rural white delegates tried unsuccessfully to block Tillman's efforts to impose a literacy test for voters.[23] Conservative and black speakers played upon the fears of rural delegates that poor whites would be disenfranchised. Appeals for justice and fair elections brought a retort from a Berkeley County delegate that "We don't propose to have any fair elections. We will get left at that every time. . . . We are perfectly disgusted with hearing so much about fair elections."[24] His callousness, unfortunately, was all too typical of some white Carolinians who abandoned any pretense of honor and honesty in order to achieve public office.

Fair play for the state's black majority also went by the boards. Segregation had begun to appear in South Carolina soon after emancipation. Blacks left white churches and formed their own congregations and denominations. The Colored Agricultural and Mechanical Association sponsored an annual state fair in Columbia and encouraged county fairs. In some social situations there were segregated facilities, but in 1890 in Columbia, Charleston, and Greenville blacks frequented theaters, ice cream parlors, and stores without any hindrance.[25]

Public school expenditures for blacks and whites had been nearly equal in 1880. By 1895, the state appropriated three times as much money per white pupil as it did for blacks.[26] Following the adoption of the Constitution of 1895 and the United States Supreme Court's 1896 decision in *Plessy v. Ferguson,* South Carolina's General Assembly passed a series of Jim Crow laws.

Not all white Carolinians accepted the idea that Jim Crow was a good idea. As late as 1897, a Charleston newspaper had editorialized: "The common sense and proper arrangement, in our opinion, is to provide first class cars for first class passengers,

The Neptune Volunteer Fire Department in Greenville was an all-black organization. *Courtesy South Caroliniana Library.*

The contrast between the Palace of Agriculture and the Negro Building at the Interstate and West Indian Exposition was a very visible reminder of the separate and not-very-equal worlds of black and white. ***Courtesy South Caroliniana Library.***

white and colored. . . . To speak plainly, we need, as everyone knows, separate cars or apartments for rowdy or drunken white passengers far more than Jim Crow cars for colored passengers."[27] Common sense did not prevail.

Within a generation, virtually all white South Carolinians had forgotten that the old pre–Civil War elite had considered squeamishness about coming into contact with blacks as a lower-class white attitude. The "better sort" loudly denounced lynching, but they quietly accepted segregation.[28] Segregation by law and custom became the order of the day.[29] The first things a young Pee Dee boy saw when he got off a train at Columbia's new Union Station were "two doors to two waiting rooms and on these two doors arresting signs, 'White' and 'Colored.'"[30] He clearly understood that caste based upon color had replaced class based upon education and economics. Soon all public accommodations from theaters to water fountains at county courthouses sprouted "white only" and "colored only" signs. The labor force in the state's growing textile industry was to be all white. Because of Jim Crow, a black middle class of shopkeepers and service personnel, patronized primarily by blacks, emerged in the larger towns.[31]

There have been attempts to downplay Ben Tillman's role in creating a segregated society in South Carolina. While the state might have been drifting toward a Jim Crow world in the 1890s regardless of him, Tillman made sure that segregation became state law. He also seldom missed a chance to exhibit his racial prejudices. In 1893, following the state's most disastrous hurricane until Hugo, he discouraged northern relief efforts in the predominantly black counties of the lowcountry. He was afraid that the distribution of food to black storm victims would attract "lazy, idle crowds" as had the Freedmen's Bureau during Reconstruction.[32]

So heavily did the mantle of segregation lay on the state that North Carolina journalist Walter Hines Page wrote after an 1899 visit to Charleston that he'd "rather be an imp in Hades than a Negro in South Carolina."[33]

The Coming of the Mills

By design, no place was more segregated in South Carolina than the cotton textile mills and the mill villages that surrounded them.[34] In 1880 the fourteen textile mills in the state employed two thousand white laborers. Thirty years later there were 147 mills with forty-five thousand employees scattered across the Piedmont, and South Carolina was second only to Massachusetts in cotton textile production.[35] There was a major difference between these late-nineteenth-century mills and earlier ones. Whereas the older mills had produced only yarn, the newer ones produced cloth or manufactured goods.[36] The rapid growth of the state's textile industry was not unlike the boom times of midwestern and western towns a half century earlier. Yet, as one observer lamented, South Carolina's burgeoning textile industry was "a mere adjunct of a New England-dominated industry."[37]

Industrialization was welcomed, albeit with some uneasiness, by a still predominantly rural society that for more than two centuries had exalted the plantation ideal and looked down on those "in trade."[38] The argument that usually won over the traditionalists was one that appeared in Grace Lumpkin's *The Wedding*, a novel set in Columbia in 1907. After listening to a Confederate veteran decry the growth that was destroying his city's "dignity and traditions," a friend replied: "The young men can grow up with the city and prosper with the city. It will benefit your own sons."[39] It was an argument most Carolinians, struggling to get ahead, found difficult to refute.

The Columbia Duck Mill, one of the country's first electric-powered textile mills, was located on the banks of the Congaree River. The mill workers lived across the river in a company-owned town. *Courtesy South Caroliniana Library.*

Local boosters wanted mills in their towns as signs of "progress." And they did more than just talk. They put up their hard-earned capital. Initially, the mills were locally owned and operated. As the textile industry continued to expand, northern capital entered the scene, but outside investors were careful to allow local individuals to continue to manage the mills.[40]

The mills produced a new working class. They had to. There was no concentration of population in the towns of the Piedmont. Workers—or "operatives," as they were called—were recruited from all over the rural upstate. Removed from the soil, these former yeoman farmers and tenants became, like their fellow Southern mill workers, a "cracker proletariat." They were not well suited to the regimentation of mill life.[41]

The long day for workers began when they arose at 4:30 A.M. and usually ended when they went to bed at 9:00 P.M. Until state law reduced the work week to sixty hours in 1907, the standard work week was sixty-six hours: twelve hours a day Monday through Friday and six hours on Saturday. There was time off for workers to go home for their meals. In many a Piedmont town, the mill's whistle became the standard time for the entire community.[42]

Local boosters might want mills because that was an indication of the community's progress, but they did not want to associate with the workers. As early as 1889, an upcountry newspaper editor warned about creating a "caste between our own race."[43] His warnings went unheeded. It was no accident that in Columbia the mills initially were located outside the city limits, or that in Union the mill district was separated from the town by the width of a street. Which side of the street you were from established your standing in the community.[44] "Mill Hill," "bobbin dodger," and "lint head" became pejorative additions to most townspeople's vocabulary. The slurs made it quite evident to the operatives that Tillman's white supremacy did not mean white equality.

A Divided Electorate

The constitution of 1895, combined with a series of election laws and intimidation, effectively eliminated black participation in South Carolina politics. With blacks no longer a factor, there was little unity among the white population. Tillman's predominantly rural following was just one faction. The Conservatives joined forces with the growing middle class of upcountry towns; this alliance appeared at the same time as the national Progressive movement and exhibited many of the characteristics associated with progressivism. The third faction, the mill workers, did not emerge as a political force until after 1900. Mistakenly, many have lumped the mill operatives into Tillman's fold. This was not so. Tillman was a farmer through and through and spoke contemptuously of the "damned factory class."[45] Ironically, one of Tillman's chief supporters, Coleman L. Blease of Newberry, emerged as the operatives' spokesman. These three groups—Tillmanites, Conservatives/Progressives, and Bleaseites—jockeyed for power within the folds of the Democratic party. The party's primary, instituted in 1896, became more important than the general election.

The Blease Phenomenon

Cole Blease was one of Tillman's earliest and most ardent disciples. However, unlike his political mentor, he did not dismiss the mill workers as beneath contempt. In them, along with the downtrodden tenant farmers, he found a constituency.

South Carolina society was going through a fundamental reorganization. The independent yeoman farmer was disappearing. As individuals lost their farms due to taxes or debts, they either became tenants or mill operatives. They were a new class of dispossessed.[46] They were highly individualistic, suspicious of government and reformers, and resentful of the disdain with which they were treated as less than equal citizens. "You think we were laid by a buzzard in a hollow stump and hatched by the sun," said one ardent Bleaseite. And another said, "I know I ain't goin' to vote for no aristocrat." This class antagonism had been fueled by comments such as "You can tell a crowd of Bleaseites as far as you can see them."[47] Even more than Tillman, Blease appealed to prejudices of class and race. However, looking past the vicious rhetoric, one finds the cries of people struggling to maintain their dignity against what they saw as overwhelming and impersonal forces.[48]

In 1910, after two unsuccessful statewide races, Blease was elected governor with the virtually unanimous support of the mill workers and liquor and gambling interests. Aristocratic Charleston supplied him with his margin of victory. Voters there seemed to back anyone who wouldn't interfere with their racetrack, gambling, and drinking habits.[49] Blease's view was that if an individual wanted to drink or gamble, that was his or her affair, not the state's.

In the first editorial cartoon ever published in a South Carolina newspaper, *The State* depicted Coleman L. Blease as a vulture threatening to attack the virtue of South Carolina. Many political observers credited a voters' backlash to this cartoon as instrumental in Blease's 1910 victory. ***Courtesy South Caroliniana Library.***

During his two terms as governor, he opposed anything that he viewed as a threat to family unity and individual dignity. Compulsory education was really "paid agents of the State in control of children."[50] He consistently fought any law or regulation concerning safety, wages, public health, or education.

Blease openly quarreled with the press, the judiciary, and the legislature. On more than one occasion, the General Assembly had to delete entire sections of veto messages because of the abusive and profane language they contained.[51] The governor did not care if his vetoes were overridden. He felt it his duty to exercise the veto power. He also pardoned more than fifteen hundred criminals in the state penitentiary. There were accusations that bribes had been given for some pardons, but no evidence ever pointed directly to the governor.

To many South Carolinians, even Tillman, Blease was an embarrassment. Yet, his presence in political races resulted in the highest voter turnouts in this century. In 1910, some 80.2 percent of registered voters cast their ballots,[52] "Coley" might upset "respectable folks," but he surely had a lot of friends. Bleaseism was the last hurrah of a dying world, a world in which all whites were equal and blacks were the mudsills of society. Its temporary political success shook the "better sort" in the state's towns, who made every effort to see that it would not recur.[53] When Richard I. Manning was elected governor in 1914, Blease resigned the governorship so that he wouldn't have to relinquish the office to a man whose progressive philosophy he detested.

The Progressives

The Progressive movement on the national level was a crusade for political and social reform against the evils that beset turn-of-the-century American society. The wrongs to be righted included the elimination of political bosses, improvement of public health and education, and establishment of city services.

In South Carolina there were progressives, but they were careful not to align themselves with any national reform effort, because their opponents were itching for the chance to label their ideas "foreign." The reforming impulse in the state also was tempered by the political reality that there was and would be only one political party. That fact goes far to explain the cautious nature of South Carolina's progressives.[54] South Carolina's progressive leadership began at the grass roots level, where men and women worked to make their communities better places in which to live. Across the state, local causes included improving schools, opening hospitals, creating parks and playgrounds, building water and sewer systems, and professional fire protection. These basic reforms were much needed.

As towns attracted new citizens from the countryside, stores became more specialized. In St. Matthews, the pharmacy dispensed Pepsi Cola. *Courtesy South Caroliniana Library.*

Education clearly was at the top of the list. The state's best public school system was in Charleston, although there were new ones in Columbia and several upstate towns. One newspaper editor considered a sound educational system equal to getting a new railroad or factory in boosting a town's image and promoting its growth. Another even dared to suggest that South Carolina emulate New York, Pennsylvania, and Massachusetts, whose good schools had "been the greatest blessing to the people. Why should South Carolina be behind in this respect?" Good schools would attract "progressive citizens" from the countryside and provide the educated work force necessary for economic diversification.[55]

In 1915 the small upstate community of Anderson installed electric streetcars as one of a number of progressive civic improvements. *Courtesy South Caroliniana Library.*

Private education, particularly private high schools, still played a major role in educating middle-class youth, both black and white.[56] As late as 1916, one in eight high school students was enrolled in a private school. And no wonder: in a survey of the state's schools, William H. Hand reported that there were only thirteen proper four-year public high schools in the state: Abbeville, Anderson, North Augusta, Anderson, Bamberg, Charleston (two), Darlington, Summerville, Johnston, Winnsboro, Marion, Mullins, and Bennettsville.[57]

The crusade for public education was pretty much left to individual communities and counties. There was strong opposition to compulsory education from rural and mill areas, where children were needed to help support their families.[58]

In 1900 less than one-third of the state's youth were enrolled in school. Of those who were in school, one in three attended classes for just sixty to ninety days. A decade later, at least one-half of the children in South Carolina attended school for part of the year.[59] As for higher education, in 1910 there were nineteen institutions of "recognized college grade" and six more with "College" in their names. State funds were stretched to provide inadequate support for five colleges. None of them received even regional accreditation until after 1920.[60]

Public health, like education, was an issue that progressives across the country espoused. American cities, even small ones like those in South Carolina, were unhealthy places in which to live. Sanitation in the state's cities and towns was virtually nonexistent. In Charleston pigs still foraged on vacant lots and unpasteurized milk was sold to the city's poor. After early-twentieth-century scares with typhoid and yellow fever, Charleston installed a central sewer system to eliminate twelve thousand open privies and clamped down on farm animals within the city limits.[61]

Horses, however, were not covered by the port city's animal ordinances and continued to be a major source of filth. One formula estimates one horse for every four inhabitants of a town; that horse, in an eight-hour day, would deposit twenty pounds of manure and half a gallon of urine on the city's

Buzzards, protected by a city ordinance, helped keep Charleston's city market clean. ***Courtesy South Carolina Historical Society.***

streets.[62] Thus, on a daily basis, Newberry, Sumter, and Florence each received about twelve tons of manure; Columbia, nearly 53 tons; and Charleston, more than 135 tons. It's no wonder the foot scraper was an essential item at everyone's doorstep.

While the state's larger towns tried to cope with sanitation and health problems, there was active opposition in the mill villages. In 1900 the State Board of Health termed mill villages "pest holes for the corruption of the whole State." In Union, mill owners supported their operatives, who literally fought and prevented public health officials' inoculating them against smallpox. As a result, the disease reached epidemic proportions and spread to other towns.[63] Smallpox wasn't the biggest killer in South Carolina. Tuberculosis, or consumption, was. Among the other most common causes of death were childbirth, malaria, whooping cough, measles, and diphtheria.[64]

All who called themselves progressives were concerned with improving public health, but women were particularly active in this area. Although women could not vote, they were among the most determined progressives and played a major role in many reform efforts. Women's church groups at the local level were vital to the success of the temperance movement and the campaigns for hospitals and libraries. The newly formed South Carolina Federation of Women's Clubs provided statewide support for such causes as the establishment in 1915 of the state's first tuberculosis treatment center.[65]

Although women could not vote in South Carolina until 1920, that did not stop them from supporting progressive causes or politicians. These Columbia women were photographed in Washington where they had just attended the inauguration of Woodrow Wilson. ***Courtesy South Caroliniana Library.***

The progressive era in South Carolina generally is traced to the 1903 introduction of the state's first child labor law by Richland County Senator J. Q. Marshall. He had introduced it at the insistence of a group of Columbia woman. What began as something of local interest soon became a statewide issue. Spurred on by the editorial voice of *The State*, the bill became law.[66] The campaign for child labor legislation established a pattern that was to continue for nearly two decades.

The State, now the largest newspaper in South Carolina, championed numerous progressive causes at the local and state levels. Just as important as its editorial support was its serving as a medium through which ideas could spread to other communities. By 1910 train schedules made it possible for *The State* to be in most South Carolina towns before breakfast.[67]

Reformers, as progressives tended to call themselves, considered liquor to be one of the state's major social ills. In 1907 the Dispensary was abolished, and by 1909 twenty of forty-one counties had voted to become "dry." Following a statewide referendum in 1915, South Carolina prohibited the public sale of all alcoholic beverages.

The Threat of Violence

Violence, a legacy of Reconstruction, haunted the state and threatened social stability. In 1891 a Newberry County man wrote: "Out of the nine representatives from the State on the floor of the American Congress . . . , the blood of their murdered victims drips from the fingers of four of them."[68] Ten years later, Charleston had a higher murder rate than did Philadelphia, a city fifteen times larger. Statewide there were nearly twice as many murders in South Carolina as there were in Chicago, which had a larger population.[69] A state judge termed South Carolina "an armed camp" and said: "Our young men and boys, black and white, rich and poor, seem to think their outfit is not complete without a pistol."[70]

The middle-class town folk, the heart of the progressive movement, recoiled from the violence around them. No doubt, it was reformers' reactions to brutality on the gridiron that led to the abolition of football at Wofford (1896–1914), Furman (1897–1913), the University of South Carolina (1906), and the College of Charleston (1912, permanently). The Carolina-Clemson game was not played from 1903 to 1908 following the near riot between the two student bodies in 1902.[71] But banning

The University of South Carolina football team in 1912. ***Courtesy South Caroliniana Library.***

football was one thing; attempting to stem the mayhem in their communities was another.

In towns across the state, reformers had little success with individual murders, because juries generally determined that the victims deserved their fates. Two of South Carolina's most prominent editors, Francis W. Dawson of the *News and Courier* and N. G. Gonzales of *The State*, were gunned down in broad daylight on the streets of their hometowns. Juries acquitted the defendants in both cases.

Reformers had a little better luck in trying to curb mob violence, especially lynching. For the most part, lynching was directed at blacks, especially those accused of rape or murder. After the 1890 lynching of Willie Leaphart in Lexington, "responsible whites" generally condemned lynchings. *The State* and the *News and Courier* were persistent and powerful foes of lynchings and mob violence. Nonetheless, following the 1898 race riots in Phoenix in Greenwood County, fifteen individuals became the victims of lynch mobs.[72]

In the decade after 1898, progressives seemed to be winning the battle of public opinion in support of law and order. Then Cole Blease was elected governor. He openly espoused lynching as "necessary and good." While blacks were the chief subject of his invective, he also said he would pardon any man or mob who killed a doctor who had given a physical examination to a young girl. Blease's endorsement of lynching frightened the middle class because, as the *Southern Christian Advocate* noted: "Today the negro, tomorrow the prominent attorney."[73] Lynching and Bleaseism were serious threats to progressivism and the efforts of the reformers to reshape and control their communities.

These somber Lexington County men composed the jury that acquitted Lieutenant Governor James Tillman of the murder of N. G. Gonzales, editor of *The State*. *Courtesy South Caroliniana Library.*

Lynching was an all too frequent occurrence in South Carolina despite strong editorial opposition from the *News and Courier* and *The State* newspapers. *Courtesy South Caroliniana Library.*

Richard I. Manning

From 1902 to 1918, with the notable exception of Cole Blease (1911–1915), South Carolina's voters elected men who, if they were not progressive, at least did not try to derail reform.

Under Governor Richard I. Manning, progressivism in South Carolina reached its zenith. He championed the reorganization and modernization of the State Hospital for more humane treatment of its patients. During his administrations, legislation was enacted reorganizing the corrections system, creating workmen's compensation, establishing the South Carolina Highway Department, and authorizing a local option for compulsory school attendance.[74]

Upon Governor Manning's recommendation, the South Carolina Tax Commission was created. It equalized assessments and effectively enforced the state's income tax laws. The efficient managing of the state's revenues provided the funds to pay for progressive reforms.[75]

The establishment of a state highway department was one of the numerous progressive reforms of Governor Richard I. Manning. The department then had to do the best it could with a system of unpaved roads and convict labor. *Courtesy South Caroliniana Library.*

The Mill Problem

There was a negative side to progressive reform. Reformers viewed blacks and mill workers as "unfortunates" and "children" in need of "up-lift." Working-class whites, struggling to maintain some control over their lives, greatly resented reformers as "do-gooders."[76] Especially irritating to mill workers was the blind eye that reformers turned to the actions of mill owners while blaming all of the problems of the mill villages on the workers.[77]

The mill workers' resentment gave Blease the political leverage that he needed to win public office. Progressives were dismayed that the "unfortunates" were so ungrateful. Under the guise of political reform, there was a concerted effort to reduce the political influence of the mill workers.

In Columbia (1910) and Spartanburg (1913), the city commission form of government replaced the old aldermanic system with its wards. All commissioners would be elected at large, thus diluting the influence of votes from the mill wards.[78] In 1912 John P. Grace's defeat of Charleston Mayor Robert Goodwyn Rhett led to an abortive effort to have the election annulled by instituting a commission form of government immediately.[79] The at-large method of election that was so common in South Carolina towns and counties until recently can be traced to the efforts of the progressives. They were determined that mill operatives, whom they viewed as threats to stability and progress, would have as little voice as possible in the government of their communities.[80]

A New Order

The quarter century that had begun in 1891 with the farmers' revolt against the established order ended with the triumph of middle-class town folk. Tillmanites had made their peace with the Conservatives, and elements of both factions could be found in the ranks of the Progressives. Blacks had been disenfranchised and working-class whites effectively neutralized at the local level. The resulting political power structure would remain in firm control of South Carolina for another fifty years.

A farm lake near Pelion, 1908.
Courtesy Mr. and Mrs. Clyde Fogle.

Chapter 2

A LAND OF MONUMENTS AND MEMORIES, 1916–1941

> Indeed, in every civilization worth the name there is something of the Past; not alone history, tradition, custom, and precedent, but ways of life and of thought and even of motives dictating behavior.
>
> —Archibald Rutledge, *My Colonel and His Lady* (1937)

To many Americans in the years between the world wars, South Carolina and South Carolinians were quaint relics. In 1930, in what was generally a favorable article about progress in South Carolina, the *New York Times* reported: "More than any other state of the Confederacy, South Carolina has

Charleston, South Carolina's fabled port city, was described by the *New York Times* as "a living monument." *Courtesy South Carolina Historical Society.*

seemed to the rushing industrial regions of the United States 'a land of monuments and memories.'"[1] Unfortunately, "The New Era" touted in a special edition of *The State* that had prompted the *New York Times* story turned out to be a will-o'-the-wisp.[2] Despite the efforts of newspaper editors and chambers of commerce during the 1920s and 1930s, the state and its people lived in a world where history was not past, but present.

"The War to End All Wars"

South Carolina's brief burst of progressivism culminated during the administrations of Governor Richard I. Manning (1915–1917, 1917–1919). During his second term, Manning continued to push his "program of economic and social betterment." Among the reforms enacted into law were the State Highway Commission, a school for mentally retarded children, an industrial school for delinquent white girls, and the introduction of the secret ballot for all elections. Taking his cue from President Woodrow Wilson, the governor appeared in person to deliver his annual "State of the State" address.[3]

Manning backed Wilson's reelection in 1916. In 1917 the President who had campaigned on the slogan "He Kept Us Out of War" led the United States into World War I. Domestic reform in South Carolina and elsewhere took a back seat as the defeat of the Central Powers became the nation's top priority.

Governor Manning headed the state's war effort, but support for the war was not unanimous. In Charleston, former mayor John P. Grace and his newspaper, the *American*, opposed America's entry into the conflict. Grace, an Irishman, wanted no part of helping England. Because of his anti-war editorials, the *American* was banned from the mails. Initially, some Carolinians of German descent in Lexington, Orangeburg, Newberry, and Charleston counties were not happy with having their ancestral homeland depicted as the evil empire. Eventually, though, most did support the war.[4]

The most prominent opponent of the war was ex-governor Coleman L. Blease. In a biting speech, he compared the governor with the Reconstruction regime: "Dick Manning is the worst Governor the State ever had, worse than Scott, Chamberlain or Moses, because they only stole money, and he is trying to steal the souls and bodies of your boys."[5] Blease later espoused the war, but by opposing it initially, he had committed a political blunder of the first order.[6]

The overwhelming majority of South Carolinians clearly

backed the war. Some 307,350 young men, black and white, registered for the draft; of these 54,284 were actually drafted.[7] Patriotic fund drives raised nearly $100 million. On a per capita basis, the state's financial contributions were among the highest in the nation.[8]

The war brought an increased federal presence in the state. The army established training centers at Columbia (Camp Jackson), Greenville (Camp Sevier), and Spartanburg (Camp Wadsworth). The Marine Corps facility at Parris Island and the Charleston Navy Yard bustled with increased activity. Concern for servicemen's health and morals led to federal pressure that closed down heretofore tolerated red-light districts in Charleston and Columbia.[9]

The state's national guard units were incorporated into the 30th (Old Hickory) Division that trained at Camp Sevier. Many South Carolinians were members of the 81st (Wildcat) Division and the 371st Regiment, 93rd (Negro) Division that trained at Camp Jackson. All these units saw action in France. The state's servicemen distinguished themselves on the battlefield. Of the seventy-eight Medals of Honor awarded during the war, seven went to South Carolinians.[10]

On the home front, the war brought increased prices for cotton, tobacco, and textiles. For a people who had lived in

A platoon of the 118th Regiment, 30th (Old Hickory) Division in the streets of St. Martin-Rivière, France, 18 October 1918. ***Courtesy South Caroliniana Library.***

poverty for half a century, the war-inflated prices appeared to be harbingers of a new golden age of agriculture. Farmers increased production and went on a spending spree.

When the war ended in 1918, cotton prices remained high. In early 1920 cotton seemed stable at 40 cents a pound, but six months later the price plunged to 13.5 cents. The State Commissioner of Agriculture estimated that South Carolina farmers had spent $250 million to plant the 1920 cotton crop. The drop in prices meant that cotton farmers suffered a $110 million loss.[11] Declining farm prices marked the beginning of a rural depression that the state would have to endure for nearly a generation.

The Farm Problem

There were many reasons for the collapse of the state's agricultural sector during the 1920s: overproduction, loss of overseas markets, drought, and the boll weevil. However, these factors simply made a bad situation worse. The state's farmlands were poor when compared even to those of other southern states. Farming marginal land and relatively good land that had been butchered was costly. Proportionally, in the 1920s and 1930s, South Carolina farmers had to purchase more fertilizers than their fellows in the rest of the country. By 1934, eight million acres were so badly worn out that they were declared "destroyed."[12]

Not only was the land poor, but so were those who farmed

Poor agricultural practices—especially the overplanting of cotton—butchered the land, as evidenced by this gully-ridden farm in Fairfield County. *Courtesy South Carolina State Museum.*

it. The average South Carolina farmer tilled about 15–25 acres. He called a one- or two-room frame or log building home. He had no livestock, not even pigs or chickens, and had no real vegetable garden. By 1930, more than six out of every ten farmers were tenants.[13] They moved from farm to farm in a desperate attempt to improve their plight. Ben Robertson sadly described the annual fall treks: "The roads of our State were filled with old trucks and one-horse wagons in November and December. They were our people and they had become migrants."[14]

Neither tenant nor landowner made any money during the 1920s. By the end of the decade one-third of the state's farms were mortgaged; the value of farmland and buildings had declined 54 percent; and 70 percent of all the state's farmers survived only on borrowed money.[15]

"The Draining Years on the Cotton Farms"[16]

Borrowed money made it possible for farmers to remain on the land, but only if they planted cotton. In 1910 only one cultivated acre in five was in cotton; by 1919, spurred on by high prices, every other one was. The increase in cotton acreage meant fewer acres for pastures and food crops.[17] Although the state's population in 1935 was three times what it had been in 1850, the amount of food produced remained virtually the same. South Carolina, an overwhelmingly agricultural state, had to import $70–$100 million worth of food annually. For poverty-stricken tenant farmers with little ready cash, this meant that there was less to eat.[18] The consequent increased dependence on a diet of pork, cornbread, and molasses made poorer Carolinians more susceptible to disease. During the 1920s, there was a marked increase in pellagra which was a direct result of poor diet. And, because of poor health and inadequate medical care, South Carolina had the nation's highest infant mortality rate.[19]

Nothing—not even hunger or the inexorable march of the boll weevil eastward from Mexico—seemed to be able to deter South Carolina farmers from planting cotton. Although first detected in 1917, it was several years before the pest made its presence felt. The boll weevil destroyed the sea island cotton crop of 1919, a blow from which that crop never recovered. Between 1920 and 1922, short staple cotton was hit almost as hard. In Williamsburg County, production dropped from 37,000 bales in 1920 to 2,700 in 1921. And in McCormick

Pellagra was a dreaded disease, especially among white mill workers. *Courtesy South Caroliniana Library.*

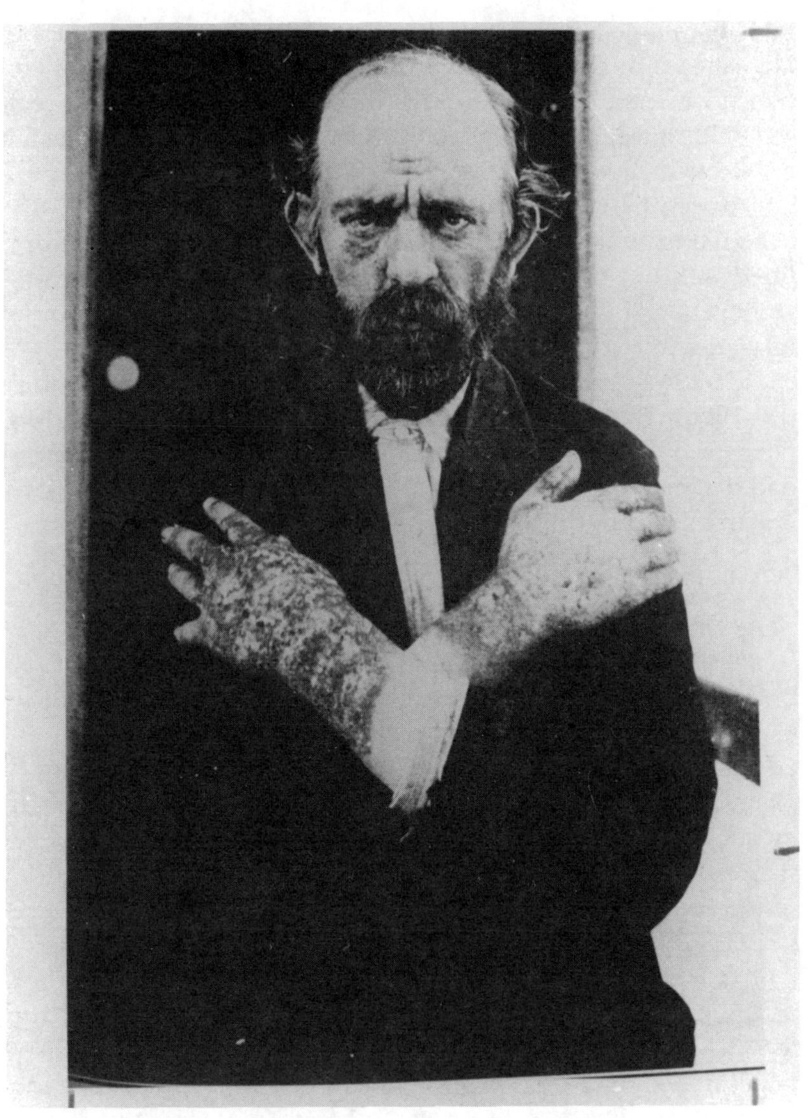

County, a farmer who'd made sixty-five bales in 1921, made only six in 1922. It is estimated that in some years the boll weevil destroyed half the crop.[20]

About the same time the boll weevil struck South Carolina, so did a series of droughts. In 1922 the state's farmers produced only 500,000 bales—a far cry from the 1,600,000 bales they'd produced two years earlier.[21] For a God-fearing people it must have seemed as if the land were cursed. It's no wonder that during the 1920s some 30,000 of the state's 188,000 farms were abandoned.[22]

Between 1920 and 1930, twenty-four of the state's forty-six counties lost population; during the next decade, eleven saw their population decline. Hardest hit were McCormick, Edgefield, Saluda, Allendale, and Abbeville. Each of these counties lost more than 15 percent of their population.[23] The agricultural depression of the 1920s stimulated a movement that had been underway since the 1890s. In an eight-month period after the disastrous harvest of 1922, more than 50,000 black farmers gave up and left the state. One of the results of this surge in black out-migration was that, for the first time since 1820, whites were in the majority.[24]

The reaction of white Carolinians to black out-migration was mixed. Some welcomed it, but others were anxious over losing a source of cheap labor. In several rural counties, whites were convinced that "outside agitators" were luring away blacks and passed laws in a futile attempt to restrict migration. While there was ambivalence about blacks leaving the state, there was genuine alarm about whites forsaking South Carolina.[25]

Although the rural populace continued to flee during the 1930s, they were not alone. By 1939, approximately 80 percent of the state's male high school and college graduates moved elsewhere in search of better opportunities.[26] South Carolinians migrated to literally every state in the union, although the general migratory pattern was northward. In 1930, there were more Carolinians living in Buffalo, Chicago,

Whether it was the 1920s or the 1930s, South Carolinians fled their cotton farms for better opportunities in the North. ***Courtesy South Caroliniana Library.***

Cleveland, Detroit, and Pittsburgh than there were in Abbeville, Beaufort, Bennettsville, Conway, or Lancaster.[27] By World War II, nearly one-fourth of the 2,266,000 people born in South Carolina lived outside the state.[28]

Hard Times in the Textile Industry

Not all of those who left their farms went to other states. Many remained in South Carolina but moved from the countryside into towns where they sought whatever employment was available. About 30,000 found jobs in textile mills.

The landscape was dotted with former "big houses" whose residents had abandoned them to tenants and sharecroppers. *Courtesy South Carolina State Museum.*

During the 1920s the textile industry expanded, and by 1925 South Carolina led the nation in the production of cotton goods. The expansion created a false image of prosperity. Except for 1923 and 1927, most firms were only marginally profitable or lost money. The war had generated huge profits which, in turn, had attracted northern investors. They purchased locally-owned mills at inflated prices and then saw the textile market founder.[29]

In an attempt to recoup their investments, the new owners brought in "efficiency experts" who recommended that mills institute the "stretch out" system. Machinery was set at the highest possible speed and workers were given a greater number of machines to tend. Workers received a small wage increase for handling twice the number of looms.[30] The "stretch out" was the most visible evidence that the new owners did not understand their workers. Townfolk and owners looked down on workers as "profligates" who had failed as farmers and were overpaid and underworked in the mills. This callousness was a serious miscalculation. The imposition of the "stretch out" led to labor unrest and strikes.[31]

In 1929 the General Assembly appointed a special committee to investigate textile workers' grievances. The committee concluded that the strikes were due to "deplorable living conditions in the villages" and "so-called efficiency measures" that put "more work on the employees than they can do." It also absolved unions of any complicity in the strikes.[32] While the legislative report was critical of management, it could do little to improve the health of an ailing industry. Overproduction and low prices led to reduced workweeks and paychecks. Overall, annual income declined. By the end of the decade, South Carolina textile workers earned the lowest wages in the industry.[33]

A Shortage of Ready Cash

In small towns merchants, bankers, and ginners found themselves with uncollectible debts and fewer customers. The agricultural crisis that began in 1920 had a debilitating effect on the rest of the economy.[34] Easy credit during the war years had led many people to overextend themselves. By the late 1920s many debtors weren't able to meet their installment payments. Town merchants organized "Pay-Up Weeks" and "Thrift Weeks." When that approach failed, some followed the lead of Greenwood merchants in publishing lists of "deadbeats." "Cash

This cotton market in Hartsville, in Darlington County, was typical of scores of others across the state. ***Courtesy South Caroliniana Library.***

and carry" became the order of the day for most small businesses.[35]

"Cash money" became scarcer as banks failed with alarming regularity. Between 1920 and 1933, more than three hundred banks closed their doors. People hoarded what cash they had or put their savings in depositories, financial institutions unique to South Carolina. Depositories generally kept a depositor's funds on hand or in a Federal Reserve Bank.[36] While numerous bank closings could be blamed on bad loans, crop failures, and undercapitalization, more than one could be traced to fraud and malfeasance. Prominent political figures, including former governor Wilson G. Harvey and former Charleston mayor T. T. Hyde, either pleaded guilty or were convicted of bank fraud.[37]

Farmers and bankers weren't the only Carolinians with money problems. By 1925, because of the agricultural depression, the state faced a two-million-dollar deficit. By 1931 the deficit was nearly five million.[38] The primary source of state revenues was a state property tax that stifled capital investment and development. Farmers paid a disproportionate share of taxes. In the mid 1920s, the General Assembly finally adopted the concept of indirect taxes. Legislators took such a fancy to this "painless" method of taxing that one critic sarcastically remarked: "South Carolina has put a tax on everything from bow legs to cuspidors." Among the luxury items taxed were tobacco, playing cards, ammunition, and certain candies. A 1925 penny tax on soft drinks made those who remained in

Life was difficult for the state's farmers, some of whom turned to truck crops in an effort to make a living. ***Courtesy South Caroliniana Library.***

South Carolina pay six cents for their "dope" while their fellow Southerners paid only a nickel.[39]

The new taxes helped fund the so-called "6-0-1" Act for education. The 1924 act was designed to aid poor school districts which historically had been underfunded. The state would pay the operating expenses for six months of the school year, if a district would pay for one month. (The "0" was for county appropriations which were not required.) The act also established minimum standards and salaries for teachers.[40]

The push for improving education came from a combination of business, political, and educational leaders. Probably the single most effective spokesperson was Wil Lou Gray, Supervisor of Adult Schools. In 1920 she had admonished the legislature that South Carolina would not "progress very much until . . . we value education, and are willing to pay for it."[41] She and other dedicated teachers made a difference as the state managed to reduce its illiteracy rate to 14.9 percent of the population. Despite South Carolina's still having the most illiterate citizenry in the country, it was an improvement worth cheering about.[42]

Boosters and Tourists

In 1923 Governor Thomas G. McLeod convened a statewide conference of community leaders to devise a strategy for promoting the state. While the "Boost South Carolina" conference's efforts were negligible, the "Wonderful Iodine State" campaign fared better. The discovery of natural iodine in South Carolina fruits and vegetables led to a successful health-oriented marketing effort for the state's produce and a publicity bonanza.[43]

South Carolina needed all the favorable publicity it could get. Every time the federal government issued statistics on the quality of life, if South Carolina didn't rank last, it was usually either forty-sixth or forty-seventh out of forty-eight states. Depending upon the category, Carolinians could give thanks for Arkansas, Louisiana, or Mississippi for keeping them off the bottom.[44]

Boosterism and community improvement were not limited to publicity campaigns. In the upcountry, local entrepreneurs supported building power plants and paving roads. By the late 1920s they had succeeded in creating the infrastructure for a modern industrial society.[45] The same could not be said for the rest of the state.

Most state highways were in such bad shape that one editor said that they "resemble the condition described in the first chapter of Genesis: 'without form and void.'"[46] That did not stop intrepid car owners from taking to the road, however. In 1912 a Swansea businessman wrote that he had driven to Columbia (a distance of about twenty miles) "and we had a rough ride on the State Road but coming back it was better for it had dried off."[47] Between 1916 and 1925 the number of registered automobiles more than quadrupled to 170,422. Congestion hit the state's towns. When Columbia installed its first traffic light in 1922, at the intersection of Sumter and

Hampton streets, a city resident protested that it was an "infringement on his personal liberty."[48] In 1929 the General Assembly passed a $65 million Highway Act to fund the construction of roads and bridges. A lawsuit challenged the constitutionality of the act, but the state's courts upheld the act's legality. The Highway Act gave the state a much-needed road network that helped all sections of the state and made possible the development of tourism as an industry.[49]

Tourism was not a new idea in the 1920s. Since the turn of the century, South Carolina resorts such as Aiken, Camden, and Summerville had been frequented by well-to-do northerners enroute to and from Florida.[50] Ordinary tourists, however, needed something to do and see, so communities created attractions. Columbia came up with the Palmafesta, South Carolina's answer to Mardi Gras; Spartanburg had an annual music festival; and Charleston launched its Azalea Festival. Folly Beach held a beauty pageant in 1928 in which "contestants were judged on the basis of complexion, hair, teeth,

A snipe boat race off South Battery during Charleston's Azalea Festival, 16 April 1937. *Courtesy South Caroliniana Library.*

The Ocean Forest Hotel opened in 1926 as part of the first serious effort to exploit what would become the Grand Strand. ***Courtesy South Caroliniana Library.***

figures, and personality."[51] Elsewhere along the coast, there were the beginnings of seaside development. In 1926, when John T. Woodside and his associates built the Ocean Forest Hotel and laid out the streets of Myrtle Beach, family resort communities already had been established at Floral Beach (Garden City), Atlantic Beach, Ocean Drive, and Cherry Grove.[52]

While most Carolinians welcomed tourists, W. W. Ball of the *News and Courier* did not: "nothing is more dreadful than tourists, whether grasshoppers, boll weevils, or money-bagged bipeds."[53] Privately, the editor of the *News and Courier* might have equated tourists with a deadly pestilence, but in print he championed the cause of historic preservation in Charleston which created a lure as attractive to tourists as a cotton square was to boll weevils.

CHERISHING THE PAST

One of the blessings of poverty was that people and governments were too poor to destroy the physical legacy inherited from previous generations. It was said that Sherman laid waste to Bamberg, Lexington, Orangeburg, Cheraw, Columbia, and other towns, but in reality his forces left a considerable number of antebellum buildings still standing. About two-thirds of the capital city's pre–Civil War structures remained after his visit.[54] In Charleston, Beaufort, and Camden, colonial and antebellum buildings survived, albeit a little worse for wear. Along country roads and in dusty little courthouse towns, physical reminders of the Old South Carolina still stood.[55]

South Carolinians had pride. Pride in family and pride in sense of place. It made no difference if one were the grandchild of planters, the grandchild of upcountry farmers, or the grandchild of slaves.[56] Individuals understood and appreciated their heritage. In Charleston, a grandmother described the intricately carved ceiling of Centenary Church: "Slaves did that wonderful work. . . . Fine people. But in slavery days they were relegated to the gallery. The white folks prayed to God downstairs."[57] In Pickens County a young man wrote: "The hills were eternal. Always they gave us strength."[58] Boys and girls growing up in the 1920s and 1930s were influenced more by their grandparents than by formal schooling. In a society that was overwhelmingly rural, personal contacts and oral traditions provided education and entertainment.[59]

Observances reflected a segregated society. Blacks cele-

Reminders of the state's antebellum past could be found in every county. This pre–Civil War dwelling was in McCormick County. *Courtesy South Carolina State Museum.*

brated holidays with special meaning for them: Emancipation Day, Decoration Day, and the Fourth of July.[60] Black expatriates, regardless of the reasons they left, still felt an "attachment for the old state that time and distance cannot destroy. After all, we love to be known as a South Carolinian."[61] Back home, however, things were different.

Public pride in the state and its past was limited mostly to whites. To them, the lowcountry had special significance. And Charleston really was the holy city: "A tiny tongue of land extending from Broad Street to the beautiful bay formed by the confluence of the Ashley and Cooper rivers is all of South Carolina that has counted in the past."[62]

While most white Southerners revered the past, Carolinians considered themselves above the rest. "South Carolinians are among the rare folk in the South with no secret envy of Virginians. They have a love for their own State which is a phalanx against all attacks of whatever order."[63] Most used the term "Carolina," not "South Carolina." In the context of their world, there was only one Carolina: "By Carolina my grandmother of course meant South Carolina—North Carolina to her and to all of the rest of kinfolks was hardly more than West Virginia."[64] There was a certain amount of provincialism

A July 4th picnic near Beaufort, 1939. Until after World War II, the Fourth was most often celebrated by black Carolinians. ***Courtesy South Caroliniana Library.***

involved in this mindset, but it contributed to the popular notion of South Carolina as a special place. Occasionally, editors might inveigh against paying too much attention to the past, but they were in the minority.[65]

The Lost Cause of the Confederacy was celebrated annually on 10 May, South Carolina's Confederate Memorial Day. The birthdays of Robert E. Lee and Jefferson Davis were public holidays. The state's schools used history texts sympathetic to the Confederacy; John H. Latane's *History of the United States* was adopted in 1927 upon the recommendation of the Sons of Confederate Veterans.[66] Special occasions, such as the 50th anniversary of Wade Hampton's Red Shirt Campaign, called for parades and speeches.[67]

Innumerable books and articles have tried to explain the cult of the Lost Cause. Few, however, have done so as well as Ben Robertson in his upcountry memoir, *Red Hills and Cotton.* "When we were growing up . . . all our older people were still grieving." In order that the state's 12,922 Confederate dead should not have died in vain, the surviving veterans and womenfolk "gave those dead young soldiers a new life in a glowing personal legend."[68] Personal remembrances were reinforced by the physical presence of "a world that had been ruined . . . a civilization that had passed."[69] That which remained of Old South Carolina seemed threatened by the clamor and hustle of industrialization.

PRESERVING THE PAST

The interwar years witnessed a growing concern for the preservation of the state's past. *The Dwelling Houses of Charleston, South Carolina* by Alice R. H. Smith and D. E. H. Smith was a pioneering work that described the architectural treasures of the port city. Three years later, in 1920, Susan P. Frost was the driving force behind the founding of Charleston's Society for the Preservation of Old Dwellings. At the Society's insistence, the city passed what became a model historic preservation ordinance.[70] And, because of the ordinance, much of Charleston's architectural heritage would be protected from the bulldozer and wrecking ball of "progress."

The Charleston effort was just one of many. Near Clemson, the Old Stone Church and Cemetery Association (1921) preserved that historic structure and in Columbia, Woodrow Wilson's boyhood home was saved by the American Legion Auxiliary (1929). The South Carolina Historical

The rear of the Heyward-Washington House in Charleston before restoration. Its condition was not atypical of much of the old city south of Broad. ***Courtesy South Carolina Historical Society.***

Association (1930) was formed to promote and encourage the study of history and the South Caroliniana Society (1937) to collect and preserve manuscripts and historical materials.[71]

Preserving the state's past took on other forms, as well. Elizabeth O'Neill Verner's etchings and prints did much to create the ambience of a Charleston at peace with the past.[72] Music faculty at Allen University collected spirituals. So did the Society for the Preservation of Spirituals.[73] It was as if Carolinians were responding with a vengeance to an article in the *Nation* in which it had been charged that they were "letting their civilization perish without resistance."[74]

But it was in written form that the most significant efforts were made to capture the past. Folklore was in its infancy, but A. E. Gonzales and E. C. L. Adams published Gullah tales and Chapman Milling wrote about the state's Indians. Histories, anthologies, articles, pamphlets, and essays appeared in almost endless succession. The sheer numbers are astounding: more than three hundred major hardbound histories and reference works specifically related to South Carolina. Even more important than the volume was the quality. Many of these books have stood the test of time and historical revision.[75]

Some were what we today would call local history, but they were first rate—and so were their publishers. The country's best university and commercial presses eagerly sought South Carolina material.[76] Among the works of this period that have become standards are Alston Deas, *The Early Ironwork of Charleston*; Asa Gordon, *Sketches of Negro Life and History in South Carolina*; Duncan Church Heyward, *Seed from Madagascar*; Helen Hennig, *Columbia*; Broadus Mitchell, *William Gregg: Factory Master of the Old South*; Elizabeth W. A. Pringle, *Chronicles of Chicora Wood*; Anna Wells Rutledge, *Artists in the Life of Charleston*; Samuel Gaillard Stoney, *Plantations of the Carolina Lowcountry*; Albert Simons and Samuel Lapham, Jr., *Charleston, South Carolina*; Leah Townsend, *South Carolina Baptists*; and David Duncan Wallace, *History of South Carolina*. Although local historians were busy across the state, lowcountry themes and titles predominated. The single most important work of the period was David Duncan Wallace's four volume *History of South Carolina*. He pulled no punches in discussing the state's past triumphs and failures and contemporary problems.

The space that Wallace and others allotted to the different periods of history indicated their relative importance. Seventy-five percent of Wallace's history was devoted to the colonial, antebellum, and civil war years. When the WPA brought out its *Guide to the Palmetto State*, 81 percent of the historical essays dealt with the years before 1865. "Modern" South Carolina didn't hold much significance for those who wrote about the state's history.

While historians were writing about the past, the state's literary community was determined to prove that "culture in the South is not merely an *antebellum tradition*."[77] The Poetry Society, founded in Charleston in 1920, nurtured some of the best writers the state has produced: DuBose Heyward, Julia Peterkin, and Josephine Pinckney. Heyward and Peterkin both achieved national acclaim for their representation of black life, but found that their portrayals displeased some white Carolinians.

Initially, white Carolinians reacted unfavorably to Peterkin's novels. University of South Carolina professor Yates Snowden dismissed them with the comment: "no Southern lady should be concerned with the Negro's fornications." In 1929 Peterkin's *Scarlet Sister Mary* won the Pulitzer Prize for Literature. Winning the Pulitzer made no difference in Gaffney, where the library banned the novel as obscene. The

Gaffney *Ledger*, however, circumvented the local censors and printed *Scarlet Sister Mary* in serial form.[78]

Race, not sex, was the reason that Heyward's collaborative effort with George Gershwin, *Porgy and Bess,* could not be performed in South Carolina. If true to the novel on which the opera was based, the cast would have to include blacks and whites. That was not permissible under Jim Crow, so South Carolinians were denied the pleasure of seeing a live local production of *Porgy and Bess* until 1970.[79]

Black and White: Slogans and Reality

When black World War I veterans who had fought "to make the world safe for democracy" returned home to South Carolina, they expected their own country to live up to its slogan. They were bitterly disappointed.[80] In January 1919 a statewide Negro Convention protested against voting barriers and segregation and asked for better schools and representation on school boards. The following May there was a race riot in Charleston sparked by white sailors' attacks on black citizens. By the time order was restored, three black Charlestonians were dead.

There was a great deal of apprehension in the state capital as whites armed themselves against a rumored "black uprising" that did not happen. Although whites prided themselves on "knowing" blacks, post-war tensions revealed that they didn't. "The race situation is bad," noted one community leader. "We don't know what is going on among the negroes and explosions may occur at any time under our feet."[81]

Meeting Street Manor and Cooper River Court were public housing projects funded by the New Deal. Rent was $4.61 per room per month. Even in a federally funded project, segregation was strictly enforced. Note the "White Application Office" sign in the lower right-hand corner. *Courtesy South Caroliniana Library.*

Within a year after the war, race relations returned to where they had been in 1917. The NAACP established chapters in South Carolina and the Charleston chapter successfully lobbied for replacing white teachers in black schools with blacks. However, the organization was viewed as so benign that in 1934 the white mayor, city clerk, and clerk of court in Darlington signed up as charter members of that city's chapter.[82] Black churches concerned themselves more with spiritual regeneration than with social causes. Black clergy denounced demon rum, but not racism. Occasionally, white clergymen, such as Episcopal Bishop Kirkman Finlay, might argue for social justice, but they were few and their impact was negligible.[83] A bulwark of the establishment, W. W. Ball of the Charleston *News and Courier*, chastised his fellow whites for having short memories: "The grandsons of the white men who could give offices to Negro Democrats in the eighteen eighties deny them now the small privilege of membership in the party."[84] His editorial comments, like the Bishop's sermons, were ignored.

While older black leaders appeared to accept the status quo, younger black men and women who grew up in South Carolina during the 1920s and 1930s had different views. They would become the elders of the state's civil rights movement during the 1950s.[85] One of those raising questions was Benjamin Mays, a native of Rambo (Epworth) in Greenwood County and professor at the Colored Normal, Industrial, Agricultural, and Mechanical College of South Carolina. He reported a conversation between two South Carolina black men: "I know my place and I stay in it," said the elder of the two men. The younger replied that he found it difficult to know what his place was, given the crazy quilt arrangement of Jim Crow laws and customs: "On the train . . . it is the front; on the ship it is below; on the streetcar it is in the rear; and in the theater, it is above." Both of the men, Mays said, were "born and reared in South Carolina," but they lived "in two different worlds."[86]

While younger black Carolinians might discuss and question the status quo with their elders, they did not do so publicly. The social order that had emerged at the turn of the century was still very much intact. That segregated world was the background for the popular, and somewhat romantic, image of South Carolina between the world wars.

These soon-to-be graduates of Mather School in Beaufort were among the younger generation of black Carolinians who would later form the core of the state's civil rights movement. ***Courtesy South Caroliniana Library.***

"OL' CAR'LINA"[87]

In 1930 the president of the American Association of Geographers cautioned his profession to learn to distinguish myth from reality when examining the American South. Then he went on to say that in examining pre–Civil War South Carolina he'd found little difference between modern myth and antebellum reality![88]

Other observers embellished the romantic image of South Carolina that began to appear with greater frequency in the national media. In a 1922 essay on Charleston that appeared in the *Nation*, visitors were urged: "Linger in these streets and lanes and gardens and enter a few shadowy interiors beyond the deep verandas that turn to the South." There they would find traces of a people who "loved dignity without ostentation, books and wine and human distinction."[89] Ludwig Lewisohn's image of "the old city that clings to the bay" could have just as easily described a movie set as the real Charleston.

There were innumerable movies with romantic Southern themes filmed during the 1920s and 1930s. However, only one, appropriately titled *Carolina*, was set in the state. In the 1934 film, Janet Gaynor and Robert Young fell in love "amidst the memory-filled plantation" where a grand Civil War ball was reenacted.[90] There were also, of course, Rhett Butler's comments about returning to his home in Charleston after the war because only there had "grace and charm" survived.[91]

A few years after *Gone With the Wind* premiered, the University of North Carolina Press published *The Springs of Virginia*, depicting "the lords of planterdom in all their glory—chiefly they were the South Carolinians."[92] That florid description, however, paled before the lyrics of popular songs about the Palmetto State. There were a dozen or more tunes with Carolina themes that appeared during this period. Of these, "Carolina in the Morning," "Carolina Moon," and "Just a Little Bit South of North Carolina" still are heard today. These and others were laments by individuals away from their Carolina homes. The images of home included clinging vines (morning glories, honeysuckle, and roses), cabins/shacks, moonlight, and dreams.[93]

Perhaps it was just coincidence, but these songs appeared at the time when Carolinians by the tens of thousands were living in northern urban environments—about as different from rural South Carolina as one could get. On a blustery December evening, someone living on the south side of Chicago or anywhere in Buffalo really might remember his "Charleston Cabin" as "heaven."[94] Locally written songs such as "Moonbeams on the Strand" and "The Azalea Waltz" tended to be a bit treacly.[95] Nevertheless, when taken as part of the total picture, it's no wonder that visitors and natives sometimes were guilty of conjuring up visions of a "camellia-scented past."[96]

The Agrarian Tradition

The internal divisions within South Carolina, upcountry and lowcountry, were very real ones. Residents of each section recognized and accepted them.[97] To upcountry folk "Charleston was a symbol. . . . It represented luxury and easy soft living and all the evils of Egypt." On an upcountry woman's tombstone was the notation: "Born 1810—Died 1890. Lived Fifty Years." The other thirty years of her life had been spent in Charleston.[98] Lowcountry folks considered upcountry folks backward: "Their civilization [is] immature. It is astonishing to observe what a large proportion of their culture was brought by low-countrymen and Virginians."[99]

Sectional differences aside, upcountry plain folk and lowcountry gentry lived in harmony with the past. They were quite

The Carolina lowcountry, with its moss-draped oaks and lazy rivers, was a world unto itself. *Courtesy South Caroliniana Library.*

The upcountry town of Spartanburg prided itself on its bustling commercialism. *Courtesy South Caroliniana Library.*

contented for their rural lifestyles to continue forever. They abhorred the concept of the "New South." Ben Robertson's Pickens County grandfather "was afraid of the power of the great factory, afraid of the wealth it accumulated in the hands of the few."[100] And Archibald Rutledge at home along the Santee damned "the modern boasted progress of the South . . . for no material greatness can ever satisfy the heart."[101]

Some Carolinians believed that the Depression had vindicated the agrarian ideal, that the "country is swinging from the Hamiltonians to the Jeffersonians. . . . The trend is toward the old ideal of Virginia and Carolina."[102] Ironically, these South Carolinians found soul mates in rich Yankees who "discovered" the beauty and serenity of the lowcountry. In one three-week period in 1925, more than one million acres of lowcountry real estate changed hands.[103] In Georgetown County at the turn of the century there were thirty-eight major plantations. All were owned by Carolinians and all but one by county residents. By World War II, wealthy northerners had purchased more than half of them. Throughout the lowcountry, 159 plantations were owned by out-of-staters as retreats or hunting lodges.[104] It also became chic to own a Charleston townhouse, "South of Broad," of course.

DuBose Heyward disapproved of the changes being wrought in Charleston in the name of progress and preservation. In *Mamba's Daughters*, he denounced the "new people" who took over the old houses, purchased antiques, and learned to say "gyarden" and "cyar."[105] Heyward, Robertson, and Rutledge, like the Vanderbilt Agrarians, took their stand for the personal world of their grandfathers against the impersonal world of progress. And they, too, lost.

Good hunting attracted many wealthy northerners to Georgetown County, where they purchased rice plantations for country retreats and hunting clubs. ***Courtesy South Caroliniana Library.***

"South Carolina Upon a Pedestal"[106]

Carolinians concerned with preserving their traditional values fought a losing battle against the "new morality" of the Jazz Age. In 1927, when John G. Richards was inaugurated as governor, he vowed that his administration would have "one great purpose . . . to place South Carolina upon a pedestal where she can be proclaimed by the world as a leader in righteousness."[107]

With the support of the General Assembly and the public, Richards was able to stamp out gambling.[108] He was less successful in eliminating other vices. Prohibition might be the law of the land, but it was violated with impunity in South Carolina. Bootlegging and rum-running flourished during the 1920s. It was estimated that between twenty-five and forty thousand Carolinians were connected with the illegal liquor trade. When the repeal of prohibition was placed before the Democratic National Convention in 1932, Charleston Mayor Burnet Maybank leaped over two other delegates, grabbed the state's standard, and participated in a twenty-five minute riotous pro-repeal demonstration.[109]

Governor Richards didn't have much luck suppressing bootlegging, but he did stand foursquare behind the enforcement of the state's blue laws. Businesses were supposed to be closed on Sunday. Period. He announced his intention to adhere to the letter of the law and then followed up his pronouncements with action. Aiken, one of the state's resort communities, didn't pay much attention to what Richards said. So the governor closed down stores and golf courses, arrested golfers, and sent shoppers flocking to Augusta. The *News and Courier* commented that Aiken was a town "where Sunday golfers are arrested, but lynchers are not."[110] The governor caught a great deal of grief for his efforts, but clearly others in the state agreed with his policies.

In Greenville a couple was sentenced to an eleven-dollar fine or thirty days in jail for "kissing while in an automobile on a principal street." A Saluda County judge was convinced that swimming pools were the "tools of the devil" and that the drought and boll weevil were God's punishment for "a state where swimming pools are permitted."[111]

The state's churches played a leading role in the efforts to protect traditional moral values. Fundamentalists attacked the curriculum in high schools and colleges and in 1927 tried unsuccessfully to outlaw the teaching of evolution.[112] While the churches may not always have been victorious in their attempts to retain traditional social values, they still were a force to be reckoned with. Membership remained strong, but the number of churches declined. Between the wars nearly twenty-four hundred rural congregations disappeared—victims of out-migration, financial difficulties, and paved roads. Seven out of every ten Carolinians belonged to a church. A greater percentage of South Carolinians were church members than in any other state except Utah.[113]

The new highway system made it possible for rural residents to attend revivals in the larger towns. Aimee Semple McPherson, Billy Sunday, and Railroad Spinks all preached to large crowds. The Gaffney *Ledger*, reporting on Spinks's crusade, said that he "cuts the right of way and lays the steel and then shouts the praises to God as he watches the gospel train transport souls from darkness to light."[114] In 1923, on Sunday's second visit to the state, the General Assembly declared 28 February as "Billy Sunday Day."[115]

Lawmakers were not as agreeable when it came to passing legislation for the benefit of South Carolina women. There was almost no support for the Nineteenth Amendment. *The State* was the only newspaper that even discussed the issue, and it opposed women's suffrage.[116] Once the Nineteenth Amendment became law, the General Assembly passed a law giving women the right to vote. Simultaneously, they excluded women from jury duty. Legislators thought "respectable women had no real desire to be jurors" and that it was their duty to "protect" the weaker sex from "the unpleasantness of jury duty."[117]

When women really needed protection, the legislature turned a deaf ear. Women's groups repeatedly lobbied "to protect their sex by requiring medical inspection of prospective husbands." It made no difference that South Carolina had one of the highest rates of venereal disease in the country.[118] The General Assembly had no intention of interfering with the time-honored double standard.

The Great Depression

The stock market was the last thing most Carolinians had on their minds on 24 October 1929. It was Big Thursday! Clemson was undefeated and the University of South Carolina had only one loss coming into the game. Both teams looked like solid contenders for the Southern Conference championship. Fourteen thousand fans jammed the old wooden stadium at the Fairgrounds to see Clemson break a tie and win 21–14.[119]

Aiken County women were among the most active in the state's small women's suffrage movement. On 26 January 1917 they staged a parade to publicize their cause. ***Courtesy South Caroliniana Library.***

It took a few days for the news from New York to sink in, but when it did. Big Thursday 1929 also happened to be Black Thursday. If Carolinians had thought that things couldn't get any worse after the agricultural crisis of the early 1920s, they were mistaken. And no sector of the economy was hit harder than agriculture.[120] Cotton prices went even lower. By June 1932, cotton was bringing 4.6 cents a pound, its lowest price since 1894. It managed to climb back up to 6 cents in early 1933—if a buyer could be found. Annual farm income dropped from $735 in 1929 to $216 in 1933.[121]

Bank failures were nothing new, but now major financial institutions began to go under. On 31 December 1931, People's State Bank, with forty-four branches, closed. Frantic depositors, fearing the loss of their funds, began runs on otherwise sound banks. South Carolina National Bank was kept afloat in January 1932 by $500,000 cash flown in from Charlotte.[122] In Walterboro, two armed men broke into a closed bank and took the amount of money that they had on deposit. They buried their cash in a safe place and turned themselves in to the sheriff. When tried, the jury refused to convict them and they became folk heroes.[123]

State government did little or nothing. Everyone seemed

willing to wait and see what Uncle Sam would do. Governor Ibra Blackwood's 1933 "State of the State" address could have been ghostwritten by Herbert Hoover. Balancing the budget and slashing expenditures for education were its main themes.[124] It was not until 1937 that the General Assembly enacted any assistance for old-age pensioners, the blind, and dependent children. Opponents of social legislation had blocked it by saying that the state's constitution permitted pensions only for Confederate veterans, their widows, and faithful slaves.[125] Meanwhile, state employee salaries were reduced and what was left was paid in state scrip. City governments in Charleston and Columbia also resorted to scrip.[126]

There was no social safety net. Unemployment in Charleston was 20 percent; in Richland County it was 44 percent. In 1931 Columbia charities served nearly half a million free meals; in 1932 the number jumped to over seven hundred thousand. The Columbia *Record* reported Carolinians literally starving to death and more than a hundred poor souls living in the city dump behind Elmwood Cemetery.[127]

The times were hard. As Mamie Fields, a James Island teacher, noted: "Those who had nothing much went down to nothing. I won't forget what one little boy told me when I was asking each child what he wanted Santa Claus to bring. He said, 'I want an orange.'"[128]

The New Deal in South Carolina

Hunger. Starvation. These were terms that South Carolinians generally associated with the masses in Africa or Asia. In May 1933 Congress created the Federal Emergency Relief Administration to provide grants to the states for food, clothing, and work relief. By the end of the summer, one-fourth of the state's population was on relief.

The South Carolina Emergency Relief Administration (SCERA) was an "administrative nightmare." In some counties, favoritism, nepotism, and incompetence tainted relief efforts. Efficient management was hindered by the absence of any state or local relief/welfare program on which to build. Although sometimes criticized, "the SCERA became for thousands of South Carolinians the difference between existence and starvation."[129]

The school lunch program of SCERA made a big difference in the life of one young South Carolinian: "I'm so glad you started lunches at school. [My brother] Jim and me have to take it by turns at home; one morning he has breakfast and the next morning I eat. But like I told Jim this morning; he won't have to be hungry long cause at 12 o'clock he'll get a bowl of hot soup."[130]

The Civilian Conservation Corps (CCC) was as popular as SCERA was unpopular. Young men between the ages of seventeen and twenty-five were eligible to participate in the program in six-month stints for up to two years. For their labors, the youths were paid thirty dollars a month, twenty-two of which were sent home. By 1939, nearly thirty-two thousand young men had worked in the thirty camps scattered across the state. Much of the work they did was conservation-oriented. The state park system developed out of CCC projects.[131]

The Works Progress Administration (WPA) and the Public Works Administration (PWA) transformed the face of South Carolina.[132] The agencies employed local workers to build highways, bridges, schools, water and sewer systems, libraries, courthouses, and airports. The largest project in the state, and one of the largest in the country, was Santee Cooper.

In 1934 the General Assembly created the South Carolina Public Service Authority (commonly called Santee Cooper) with the power to produce and sell electricity; develop inland navigation along the Santee, Cooper, and Congaree rivers; reclaim swamps; and reforest watersheds. After intensive lobbying by South Carolinians, President Roosevelt gave his personal approval to federal funding for the project. Legal challenges held up construction until May 1939. In less than three years, the land that would become Lakes Marion and Moultrie was

Poinsett State Park in Sumter County had its beginnings as a CCC work camp. ***Courtesy South Caroliniana Library.***

The powerhouse for the Santee Cooper project was constructed near Moncks Corner in Berkeley County. The entire Santee Cooper project was completed in less than three years. *Courtesy South Caroliniana Library.*

cleared, dams built on the Santee and Cooper rivers, the lakes impounded, and power generated for war industries in Charleston.[133]

Less visible, but affecting more people, was the Agricultural Adjustment Act (AAA). Initially, the AAA was a program by which farmers who voluntarily took land out of production were compensated by the government. State cotton farmers were so enthusiastic about AAA that in 1933 they ploughed up more than half a million acres. Later in the decade, tobacco farmers also came under the program.[134] Cotton and tobacco acreages were reduced and allotments made based upon previous production. The AAA and other programs saved and stabilized South Carolina agriculture, but it took World War II to bring farmers a measure of prosperity.[135]

The New Deal in South Carolina primed the pump of the state's economy. The massive infusion of federal dollars—$154 million in federal loans and $258 million in grants and outright expenditures—did its job. Retail trade picked up in larger towns. The number of new motor vehicle registrations doubled. In 1930, with a per capita income of only $223, the state ranked last; by 1940 per capita income had increased to $281 and the state's ranking was forty-fifth. It was a modest gain, but an indication that things were getting a bit better.[136]

It was no accident that South Carolina received more than $400 million in federal assistance during the Great Depression. The state's political leadership was closely allied with Franklin D. Roosevelt's administration.

Women and children strung tobacco for curing in the barns. Tobacco farmers welcomed the AAA, which reduced acreages and raised prices. ***Courtesy South Caroliniana Library.***

The Political Scene

In the years after World War I, the state's political arena was relatively calm, particularly when compared to the turbulence of the preceding quarter century. Under the umbrella of the Democratic Party, a "modernized and modified Bourbonism" developed that controlled the state until the 1950s.[137]

The legislature dominated state government. Except in the case of incorporated towns, there was little local government. Counties were ruled by their legislative delegations, which controlled the budget (called a supply bill, it had to be approved by the General Assembly), set tax rates, and hired county employees. There wasn't much time spent on statewide issues. As late as 1940, 86 percent of the laws passed by the General Assembly were so-called "local bills."[138]

In the legislature a group of lowcountry politicians emerged who were determined to use state government as a "tool for economic development."[139] Included in this group that soon became a powerful force in the General Assembly were Richard Jefferies of Colleton County and Edgar Brown and Solomon Blatt of Barnwell County.

On the state level there was an interesting cast of characters. Representing South Carolina in the United States Senate were Coleman L. Blease, James F. Byrnes, and Ellison D. Smith. As a group, they and governors Olin D. Johnston and Burnet R. Maybank were better known outside the state than any political figures since the 1850s. The state's senior senator was Ellison D. "Cotton Ed" Smith, a man labeled by *Time* magazine as a "conscientious objector to the twentieth century."[140] A political orator of the old school, at stump meetings his voice could be heard more than a mile away. He continually sang the praises of "my sweetheart, Miss Cotton" and frequently wore a cotton boll in his lapel.[141]

Smith attracted national attention for walking out of the 1936 Democratic Convention in Philadelphia because a black clergyman gave an invocation. In a subsequent reelection bid, the "Philadelphia Story" became an effective campaign device: "And he started praying and I started walking, and as I . . . walked . . . it seemed to me that old John Calhoun leaned down from his mansion in the sky and whispered . . . you did right, Ed."[142] Although he was chairman of the Senate Agriculture Committee, Smith had little influence with President Roosevelt.

Jimmy Byrnes, who defeated Blease in a tough senatorial race in 1930, became the "New Deal man" in South Carolina and controlled the state's patronage. He also attended the 1936 convention, and his primary opponents pilloried him for not taking a walk as had Smith. They also attacked his support of the New Deal. Byrnes's reply was that since 1933 the state had sent only $10 million in taxes to Washington and received $240 million in return.[143] That was a message the state's voters understood and applauded. The senator was reelected handily.

One of Byrnes's protégés and allies was Mayor Burnet Maybank of Charleston, a staunch New Dealer and one of the key backers of Santee Cooper. In 1938 he shattered the myth that a Charlestonian couldn't be elected governor. On the stump, his strong Charleston brogue, rapid-fire delivery, and unnerving habit of changing subject in mid sentence, made his speeches virtually unintelligible to voters more than forty miles from the coast. However, his exuberance, sincerity, and firm control of Charleston's political machinery assured his win.[144]

Olin D. Johnston was the antithesis of the aristocratic Maybank. A self-made man, he was proud of his working-class origins. As governor he ran afoul of the legislative leadership

WPA-built sheds would soon cover most of the open-air sections of the State Farmers' Market in Columbia. ***Courtesy South Caroliniana Library.***

when he tried to take over the Highway Department. In 1935, after the General Assembly refused to remove highway commissioners appointed by previous governors, Johnston declared the terms of some commissioners over. The recalcitrant commissioners refused to abandon the offices to which they had been legally appointed. The governor proclaimed the commissioners in "rebellion, insurrection, and insurgency." He declared martial law and ordered the National Guard to occupy the Highway Department. The courts ruled against the governor and he had to back down. Unfortunately, his two-year squabble with the Highway Department put a number of PWA road projects on hold and contributed to the state's unemployment woes.[145] His actions didn't hurt him with President Roosevelt, who supported him in 1938 in an unsuccessful attempt to unseat "Cotton Ed" Smith.

South Carolina and FDR

Following the 1928 election in which Herbert Hoover had crushed Al Smith, South Carolina Democrats began to look around for a winning nominee for 1932. Franklin D. Roosevelt's election as governor of New York was one of the party's bright spots in an otherwise bleak election year.

Senatorial hopeful Jimmy Byrnes in 1928 was the first prominent state political figure to endorse FDR. Two years later Claud N. Sapp, Chairman of the State Democratic Executive Committee, helped to organize Roosevelt Southern Clubs. In 1931 State Senators Dick Jefferies and Edgar Brown and Governor Ibra Blackwood announced for Roosevelt. These men provided FDR with a solid base of support in the state. At the Chicago convention in 1932 they actively campaigned for their candidate. Byrnes, now a U.S. senator, was particularly effective in back-room negotiations leading up to the nomination.[146]

Back home, the state's newspapers not only urged voters to support Roosevelt, they mocked Hoover and his slogan, "Prosperity is just around the corner." In an editorial the Lexington *Dispatch News* suggested that perhaps the country should "abolish corners. Then prosperity will have to show itself." And Camden's *Wateree Messenger* commented: "from where we are standing it is as dark as the inside of a bull frog's belly and sounds just as doleful."[147] South Carolina voters needed little prompting. Roosevelt won 98 percent of the votes cast. This was his greatest margin of victory in any state.[148]

When Congress convened in March 1933 for a special session, four members of the state's congressional delegation played prominent roles in the legislation passed. In the Senate, it soon became quite clear that Byrnes was one of the administration's point men. Smith cooperated with the administration, although a bit reluctantly; however, without his cooperation, it would not have been possible to pass the AAA. In the House, Congressman Hampton P. Fulmer of Orangeburg helped guide the AAA through the lower chamber and Representative John J. McSwain of Greenville was the co-author of the Tennessee Valley Authority legislation.[149]

No sooner was the "100 Days" over than W. W. Ball and the *News and Courier* "declared war on the New Deal." Oblivious to the poverty all around him, he saw no need for any of the new federal programs. His solution was to have farmers plant vegetable gardens and to send the urban poor to the countryside where they, too, could live off vegetable gardens. *The State* dismissed Ball's "rantings" as "silly" and in an editorial praised FDR as America's "Providential Leader."[150]

In 1936 Carolinians rejoiced at Roosevelt's reelection, but

Not all New Deal projects were bricks and mortar. Federally funded programs made possible canneries in each of the state's forty-six counties. *Courtesy South Caroliniana Library.*

Mayesville native Mary McLeod Bethune was director of the Negro Division of the National Youth Administration. On this visit to South Carolina she addressed students at Shanklin School in Beaufort County. *Courtesy South Caroliniana Library.*

during the second term, their support wasn't as wholehearted as it once had been. The president's attempts to pack the Supreme Court, advocacy of the Fair Labor Act, and concern for minorities alienated voters.[151] In 1938 he urged the election of congressmen who would support his programs. "Cotton Ed" Smith was not one of FDR's men. The President's attempt to meddle in a state election backfired and the senator was reelected.[152]

The key to the cooling of the state's enthusiasm for the New Deal was Senator Byrnes's lack of enthusiasm for certain programs, especially the Fair Labor Act and anti-lynching legislation. The senator was a molder of public opinion and let his views be known. *The State*, the president's most ardent newspaper voice in South Carolina, began to change its tune after W. E. Gonzales died in 1937. In 1938, in an editorial entitled "Let's Liquidate the Alphabet," *The State* called for the dismantling of the New Deal."[153] Perhaps in Columbia there might not be a need for some of the federal programs, but Columbia was a special case. The reactivation of Camp Jackson as Fort Jackson in 1939 eliminated the most visible signs of the Depression in the capital city.[154]

As the possibility of war grew, Byrnes and others who had become disenchanted rallied to the president. In 1940, Roosevelt won his unprecedented third term. Ninety-five percent of those South Carolinians who voted cast their ballots for FDR.[155]

Most Carolinians remembered very distinctly where they were when they heard that Pearl Harbor had been bombed. In the hills of Pickens County, Ben Robertson recalled that December 7th was a bright, windy day. When he and his kinfolk heard the news, they gathered as a family: "We were in trouble and our country was in trouble, and as always whenever there was trouble, we found that automatically we had come together. . . . My cousin Billy said he was ready to go. So did my cousin George. So did J. B., Mary's nephew. We went alone to the cotton fields. There before us stood the hills. . . . The hills were eternal. Always, they gave us strength."[156] A year after he wrote those words, Ben Robertson was dead. He did not live to see his grandfather's fears become reality as forces unleashed by World War II irrevocably altered the South Carolina he knew.

Chapter 3

IGNITED BY WAR, 1941–1966

> South Carolina's government is basically sound and it is friendly towards industry. Our government, our communities, and our people want industry and want to see that it is prosperous and happy. No state and no people can offer more.
>
> —James F. Byrnes,
> State Development Board *Annual Report, 1950–1951*

World War II, like the Civil War seventy-five years earlier, was the catalyst for change in South Carolina. Prior to 1941, the state did have a manufacturing sector, but it was primarily devoted to the processing of cotton. The war brought in new industries that employed large numbers of workers and increased the state's tax base. First local business and civic leaders and then state officials began to woo northern industrialists. As the regional competition for new industries increased, the state's leadership began to be concerned with presenting a progressive image to the rest of the nation. This concern, in the 1960s, would manifest itself in educational and social changes that would have been unthinkable in 1941.

WORLD WAR II

World War II did what the New Deal could not do. It brought full employment to South Carolina. The Japanese attack on Pearl Harbor accelerated the military buildup that had begun by 1940. By the tens of thousands, South Carolinians entered the armed forces. By 1945 more than 184,000 men and women were in uniform. Thousands more were not because of illiteracy or poor health. The rejection rate for black Carolinians was 56.6 percent and for whites it was 33.9 percent.[1] These rates were among the highest in the nation and were an indication of the poverty in which the majority of the state's citizens lived.

With so many able-bodied men in uniform, there was a

In 1942 President Roosevelt inspected troops at Fort Jackson, one of the country's primary infantry training centers. The visit was top secret and South Carolinians didn't know about the president's visit until several days after the event. ***Courtesy South Caroliniana Library.***

shortage of labor for farms and factories. Textile mills operated in three shifts around the clock. In Charleston nearly one hundred thousand workers labored in the Charleston Navy Yard, the Charleston Shipbuilding and Drydock Company, and other industries.[2]

The wartime payrolls brought in $100 million to the Charleston area. Retail sales doubled, and so did the number of passengers on the city's buses. Local merchants, however, saw no need to expand, because they figured that the workers wouldn't remain after the war. They were more than willing to take the laborers' money, but they tended to treat them disdainfully. Price gouging, especially for housing, was common.[3]

Numerous workers commuted fifty to seventy miles one way every day. Others paid exorbitant prices for "hot beds," where they slept in shifts. A Navy Department investigation determined that lack of housing and substandard housing hindered productivity and cost the navy at least one destroyer a month.[4] As a result of the navy's investigation, the U.S. Housing Administration subsidized the building of five thousand housing units. It also opened a rent control office and threatened to commandeer private housing. These seemingly heavy-handed actions were deemed necessary to support the nation's war effort.[5]

Although the wartime spotlight was often on the state's manufacturing sector, the majority of South Carolinians still worked on farms. As a result of losing workers to the armed forces and to better-paying jobs available in mills and defense industries, farmers were shorthanded. In an attempt to maintain and increase production, they worked longer hours and employed women and children in the fields more often.

In order to boost farmers' morale, the Department of Agriculture staged a "Farming for Victory" celebration in Orangeburg in December 1942. It included a two-mile parade, speeches, military band concerts, Thanksgiving services, and a picnic dinner. A host of civilian and military dignitaries attended. After it was all over, the United States Department of Agriculture announced that the Orangeburg celebration would be used as a model for similar events across the country.[6]

South Carolina farmers did produce bumper crops, but that didn't necessarily result in more food for the civilian population. Rationing became an accepted facet of everyday life. The ration cards and the variation in points assigned to seasonal produce were sometimes confusing, but housewives learned to make do. More than two hundred commercially processed foods were rationed, as were sugar, red meat, and coffee. Butter, tea, and chocolate were scarce. "One can to a customer" signs appeared on grocery shelves. Shoes and gasoline also were rationed, but electricity was not.

Thanks to Santee Cooper, South Carolina had enough electricity to supply lowcountry military installations, industries, and civilian customers. At night, though, a visitor might have suspected a power shortage because coastal towns were dark. Blackouts were in force for most of the war.[7]

Blackouts and overcrowding were inconveniences, but inflated food prices hurt Carolinians with limited incomes. The state Department of Agriculture maintained a price check on sixty-six food items. In January 1941, the average cost of these items was $11.51. One year after Pearl Harbor, prices had risen 41 percent. A pound of bacon increased from 28 to 40 cents; a dozen eggs from 33 to 52 cents; fifteen pounds of potatoes from 4 to 6 cents; and a pound of lard from 9.5 to 18 cents. Interestingly, the greatest price increases occurred in the farming communities of Beaufort and Orangeburg. Urban Greenville had the lowest. By the time the Japanese surrendered in September 1945, food cost 66 percent more than it had prior to the war. These higher food costs came about

Worker participation in the armed forces was recognized at Winnsboro Mills by the raising of the Army/Navy "E" flag. ***Courtesy South Caroliniana Library.***

despite price controls. In the five years after the war, without controls, they would jump another 70 percent.[8]

Coming Home

Unlike the federal government, which appeared to avoid making hard decisions about reconverting the nation to a peacetime economy, South Carolina at least gave some thought to the problems of demobilization. In 1945 the state published the results of a survey that it had conducted of South Carolinians in uniform.[9]

Among other things, the survey confirmed that Carolinians had an attachment to place. Nine out of ten soldiers surveyed said that they intended to return to their home counties. Nearly half of them wanted assistance in improving their educations—from vocational training to a high school diploma to a college degree. "Good schools for country children, white and colored, sorely needed," commented one soldier.[10] In a sad commentary on the state's colleges and

While the state made preparations for returning veterans, not all came back, as witnessed by this 1945 presentation to Gold Star Mothers in Columbia. *Courtesy South Caroliniana Library.*

universities, 40 percent of those desiring a college education indicated that they intended to go to school out of state.

The soldiers' answers caused grave concern in some government circles. And the concern wasn't that so many wanted to go to college out of state, but rather that so many soldiers were coming home. In 1945 there were 700,000 individuals employed in South Carolina. A good many of those were in defense industries that probably would cut back or cease production with the coming of peace. The state faced the possibility of having to absorb 184,000 servicemen and women into the civilian work force. While there was a lot of worrying, not a whole lot was done. At least one high school in each county established programs for veterans without diplomas.[11] However, since the schools were segregated, where there was only one high school program, it was for whites only.

Although the survey was color-blind, specific comments should have caused people to realize that black Carolinians weren't going to quietly resume their prewar roles in society. "Make definite plans to give the Negro soldier or veteran equal opportunity," was one comment. Another wrote: "South Carolina should compose a bigger and better system for both white and colored, through which the race problem can be settled."[12]

Black soldiers weren't the only ones who realized that segregation exacted a price. In 1944, a young white graduate of the Opportunity School wrote a bitter letter in which he noted that South Carolina was one of only two states that didn't permit their servicemen to vote by absentee ballot. He correctly surmised that the reason was to keep blacks from voting. "It seems to me," he asserted, "that the average [white] South Carolinian is so afraid that the negro will get ahead that he is willing to sacrifice his own rights just to make sure that the negro won't have any."[13]

The Sky Didn't Fall

The young white soldier who was angry that he couldn't vote clearly knew his state. Just a few months before he wrote his letter, Governor Olin D. Johnston had called the General Assembly into special session. His actions were a response to the U.S. Supreme Court's ruling that blacks could not be kept from voting in Texas's all-white Democratic Party primary.

South Carolina was the first southern state to respond to this attack on segregation. In April 1944, when the legislature convened, 147 bills were introduced to repeal two hundred laws relating to the conduct of primaries. "The South Carolina Plan," as it soon was called, was based upon the premise that if the state let political parties hold primaries as private organizations, then the primaries would be beyond the reach of the U.S. Supreme Court.[14] With a speed that amazed veteran legislative observers, the lawmakers enacted 147 laws in the six-day special session. The following November, the voters overwhelmingly approved the necessary constitutional amendments.

There the matter stood until 1947, when black voters in Richland County challenged the "South Carolina Plan" in federal court. Judge J. Waties Waring of Charleston heard the case. He came from one of the lowcountry's oldest families, and his decision shocked the state.

In a sharply worded opinion he ruled that the state's attempts to turn the political process over to a private organization was "pure sophistry." He chided his fellow Carolinians for denying blacks the opportunity of voting in primaries as they did in other states: "I cannot see where the skies will fall if

Governor Olin D. Johnston in a mule-drawn carriage on the way to his second inauguration in January 1943. *Courtesy South Caroliniana Library.*

On 10 August 1948, following Judge Waring's decision, black Carolinians stood in line for hours in the Waverly Section of Columbia to get the chance to vote in the Democratic Primary. ***Courtesy South Caroliniana Library.***

South Carolina is put in the same class." "It is time," he said, "for South Carolina to rejoin the Union."[15] There ensued a great deal of rhetoric and some halfhearted attempts to keep blacks out by requiring all who voted in primaries to take an oath that they would "support the social, religious, and educational separation of the races." In 1948, Judge Waring threw out the oath and the white primary was history.

In April 1948 blacks voted in a Columbia city primary, and in the following August thirty-five thousand blacks voted in the state Democratic Primary. Laws governing primaries were reenacted, but nothing was done to prevent discrimination or intimidation. Blacks could vote—and they did—but never in large numbers and seldom in predominantly black counties where their political potential was greatest.

“Killbillies” and “Opera in Greenville”

The war had made South Carolinians aware for the first time in several generations that what the rest of the country thought about them was important.

In 1944 Governor Olin D. Johnston used the negative publicity that Senator “Cotton Ed” Smith had generated as the basis for defeating one of the state’s political institutions. Johnston blamed Smith’s outspoken racism for the Supreme Court’s decision overturning the white primary. Ironically, the governor’s special session of the General Assembly that created the “South Carolina Plan” resulted in a mocking *Newsweek* article entitled “Killbillies.” That, however, was beside the point. Johnston lambasted Smith’s rhetoric, which the governor said pictured “South Carolina and the people of the South as an uncivilized race.”[16] Johnston was himself a staunch segregationist, but he successfully convinced the voters that he would project a better image of South Carolina in the U.S. Senate.

The handling of the Willie Earle lynching in Pickens County was an indication that even in a segregated society, some things would no longer be tolerated. On 16 February, 1947, Willie Earle, a young black man from Pickens County, was arrested and charged with the murder of Thomas Brown, a Greenville cab driver. The next day, a mob broke into the Pickens County jail, seized Earle, and lynched him outside of town. Although the mob actually shot, stabbed, beat, and mutilated the victim, the term “lynching” was used.

The FBI and State Law Enforcement Division launched an investigation that led to thirty-one arrests. Governor Strom Thurmond urged the vigorous prosecution of those accused of the lynching. Confessions were obtained, but they were thrown out in court and without them the jury acquitted the defendants.

The trial attracted national media attention—not, however, because it was a gruesome murder or because the jury returned a verdict of not guilty. The trial of the thirty-one white men in Greenville was a media sensation simply because it occurred at all. In a Deep South state, authorities had arrested and prosecuted individuals for what some white Southerners had heretofore considered a “justifiable” action.[17]

Among the spate of articles that chronicled the trial, one that was reprinted several times was “Opera in Greenville,” which appeared in the *New Yorker*. Author Rebecca West described the defendants’ remorse and shame as their deeds were vividly described in open court. This lynching wasn’t swept under the rug. It was closely examined under the glare of a public trial. And it was the last lynching in South Carolina.

"The Spark of Industrial Development"

During the decade after the war, South Carolina had no formal statewide plan for industrial development. The Research, Planning and Development Board, the precursor of the present-day State Development Board, was willing to act as a go-between for communities and industrial prospects. However, the arduous task of actually recruiting new industry was left up to individual communities.[18]

Municipal efforts ranged from recruiting trips to brochures, pamphlets, and advertisements extolling the advantages of a particular town. All across the state, communities ranging in size from Charleston, Columbia, and Greenville to Allendale, Kingstree, and Ridgeland established active industry-hunting programs. Charleston's Development Board, with five full-time city employees and strong support from the city's business community, was the most sophisticated. Chambers of Commerce in Conway, Dillon, and Florence led their towns' efforts. In Allendale it was returning veterans; in Bennettsville and Pickens it was civic clubs; and in Beaufort and Ridgeland it was the Jaycees.[19]

Within nine months after the war, Charleston had attracted nineteen new companies employing 812 people. Upstate, Rock Hill landed the biggest catch of the immediate postwar years when it secured a $40 million Celanese Corporation plant.[20]

Not everyone was overjoyed with the changes in what had been the closed world of prewar South Carolina. The Columbia *Record* was concerned that most of the larger industries moving in were not "South Carolina owned," but were "branches or subsidiaries of parent organizations with headquarters out of state—usually the North."[21] The issue of local ownership aside, the newspapers decided, on balance, that the new companies were welcome because they would provide job opportunities for South Carolinians.

Some didn't want new industry at all and based their opposition on a variety of reasons. One Cheraw businessman thought that local tax exemptions which were widely used to lure businesses were "unfair to our own home-grown industries" who would then have to compete with the newcomers for labor. Along the same line, he concluded that "any industry

While many communities across South Carolina were rushing to industrialize, the Catawba Nation in York County was struggling to preserve its tribal customs and identity. Since the colonial period, the Catawbas have been known for their pottery. *Courtesy South Caroliniana Library.*

Despite the establishment of plants in rural areas, roadside fruit stands were still a familiar sight. *Courtesy South Caroliniana Library.*

Local manufacturers promoted their wares at this postwar South Carolina Products Exposition. *Courtesy Mr. and Mrs. O. Harry Giles.*

that has to be paid to come into a community is not worth having."[22]

Fear of change was another factor that led some to view industrialization as dangerous to the South Carolina way of life. One small town merchant said that he and his fellow citizens were afraid "that industrialization would end their habit of closing up businesses to go fishing whenever they pleased."[23]

In some parts of the state, especially those in which "the more thoughtful citizens have failed to take a proper interest in public affairs," development was stymied. During the mid 1950s, Spartanburg and Union counties were cited as examples of communities where "political demagogues" and an absence of local leadership had resulted in the counties leaving negative impressions with industrialists. The bottom line was that companies chose other sites.[24] As long as industrial development remained primarily in local hands, the results would be uneven. Yet, had it not been for the leadership of municipalities scattered across South Carolina, "the spark of industrial development, ignited by war," would have gone out.[25]

A Cooperative State Government

By the 1950s, it was apparent that there would be a coordinated, statewide effort to attract new industry to South Carolina. The modern State Development Board was created in 1954 to fill that need. Local communities did not abandon their own campaigns, but for the first time there was one central place in the state where an industrial prospect could obtain virtually all the information required to make a site selection.

A succession of governors, beginning with Strom Thurmond, put out the welcome mat for corporate executives.

The Governor's Mansion was no longer just the official home of the state's first family. It became a frequently used site for entertaining business prospects. When James F. Byrnes succeeded Thurmond, he was surprised that he would be called upon to help recruit industry.[26]

The General Assembly was also willing to do its part. In 1954 the state passed a right-to-work law without much opposition. That would not have been possible twenty-five years earlier. In 1956, the legislature, in a special session that cost the state's taxpayers $30,000, amended the state's alien ownership law so that non-Americans, including corporations, could own up to five hundred thousand acres of land. Previously, the limit had been five hundred acres. State and municipal tax laws were amended to entice corporate investment. On one occasion, Governor George Bell Timmerman got the South Carolina Pollution Control Authority to exempt a new industry "from the provisions of the law it would have found most burdensome."[27] This message of complete cooperation was reinforced in state publications and advertising campaigns. South Carolina was one of the most aggressive Southern states when it came to industrial recruiting.

Every now and then, this aggressiveness appeared to get out of hand. In 1955 devastating floods swept through Connecticut. Purely by chance, an official of the Development Board was in the area on a previously planned industrial recruiting mission. The coincidence of the two events resulted in a heated newspaper war of words. One Connecticut editor accused South Carolina of sending carpetbaggers north to take advantage of the state's distress. The state's governor also resorted to sectional imagery: "The South is fighting the Civil War all over again in trying to take away our industry. They're on the make."[28]

While Carolinians really didn't think of industrial recruiting as war, they did use military terms when it came to defending the state's all-important textile industry. In this instance, the General Assembly was more than willing to take on the Japanese government in a dispute over textile imports. In July 1955, U.S. trade negotiators made "deep tariff concessions" to the Japanese which would permit them to export large quantities of cheap cotton goods to this country. South Carolina textile manufacturers, legislators, and newspapers reacted as if shot. When the new trade agreement went into effect on 11 September 1955, journalists compared it to Pearl Harbor. Two months later, in an effort to stem hostile American public opinion, the Japanese government agreed to a temporary halt of the cheap exports.[29]

That wasn't enough for South Carolina legislators. In March 1956 they passed the Hart-Arthur Act requiring wholesale and retail establishments selling textiles made in Japan or goods made from Japanese cloth to display conspicuously a sign: "JAPANESE TEXTILES SOLD HERE."[30] Within a matter of weeks, merchants in Lancaster, Chester, and other towns dependent on textile manufacturing announced that they wouldn't stock any Japanese goods. When plants shut down, or there were layoffs, the press reported that the workers were on "Japanese vacations."[31]

The U.S. Department of State received a formal complaint from the Japanese ambassador. Alabama followed South Carolina's example, and it looked as if an international incident were in the making. Southern textile manufacturers received no support whatsoever from the Eisenhower administration, and one U.S. trade official in Tokyo was quoted as "regretting" South Carolina's law.[32] In September 1956 the Japanese agreed voluntarily to extend their own self-imposed textile export quotas. Governor Timmerman caustically

Textiles were the state's most important industry. This is a loom in the Hickman Mill of the Graniteville Manufacturing Company in Aiken County. ***Courtesy South Caroliniana Library.***

commented on the conclusion of the issue: "Since the government in Washington has refused to protect the welfare of our people, it is gratifying to learn that the government of Japan is not equally indifferent."[33]

"A Two-Fisted Competitive Spirit"[34]

The Japanese textile legislation was not an indication that the state didn't want to be involved in international trade. It did, as evidenced by the funds spent on improvements at the state's three ports: Beaufort, Charleston, and Georgetown. The General Assembly had created the Ports Authority in 1942 to oversee the three ports. Not much happened during the war, but in December 1945 the Ports Authority began operating the North Charleston terminals which had been managed by the military. The changes in the ports, particularly Charleston, were spectacular.

Before the Ports Authority began operations, no steamship lines had regularly served Charleston. By 1948 there were thirty-six. In the decade after the war, the value of imports increased tenfold, exports multiplied six times, and the number of ships doubled. During the 1950s Charleston was transformed from an unranked port to the fifteenth busiest in the nation. Georgetown developed into an important secondary port.[35]

In 1959 the state invested $21 million in new or improved facilities at all three ports. New docks and warehouses were built at Beaufort and Georgetown and the Ports Authority "changed the face of the Charleston waterfront."[36] A few years later, in a farsighted move, the Ports Authority began constructing its first containerized freight facilities.

The New York *World-Telegram*, concerned about the port of Charleston's growth at the expense of New York, noted that South Carolina had changed the way it did business. "In Charleston's mercurial growth is reflected South Carolina's determination to get rid of the old mockingbird and magnolia psychology in favor of an up-to-date two-fisted competitive spirit."[37]

The state's improved competitiveness didn't just happen. It was the result of careful planning and a lot of hard work. Spearheading the effort to attract new industries was the State Development Board, which was reorganized in 1959. Greenville businessman Francis M. Hipp was appointed chairman. Hipp and his successor, Columbia attorney Bratton Davis, gave the board a solid corporate image.

The General Assembly enacted so much business legislation during the 1959 session that reporters dubbed it the "Industrial Session."[38] Tax laws were revised and an airplane was purchased for the Development Board. The first annual Governor's Conference on Business, Industry, Education, Agriculture, and Government was held. Governor Ernest F. Hollings and a hundred of the state's business leaders went on an industry-hunting "safari" to New York. Subsequently, there were similar trips to Europe and South America.

In 1960, at Governor Hollings's urging, the General Assembly established a joint study committee on education. Future governors Robert E. McNair and John C. West were key members of the committee. Fewer than 5 percent of first graders would finish college, and the state's dropout rate was 50 percent. Perhaps technical education might be the answer. The act creating the state's technical education system was passed in 1961 and the first "Tech Center" opened in Greenville the following year.

One of the act's most important provisions was the special schools division whereby South Carolina would train workers for a specific industry if it located here. The company set the employee standards, but South Carolina paid for equipment and materials to train students on production lines that exactly simulated plant conditions.

The state's industrial start-up training program was "one of the pioneering responses to the need for a flexible but effective industrial training program."[39] Among the early beneficiaries were Lockheed, Smith Corona Marchant, and Firestone. They and other industries that located in South Carolina loudly sang its praises. Capitalizing on the good national publicity, the Development Board ran an effective promotional campaign, "Start Up in the Black."[40] Other Southern states soon followed suit, but South Carolina's innovative program contributed significantly to the remarkable industrial growth that came to pass during the 1960s.

Industrial development transformed South Carolina's economy. Almost every postwar year saw astounding gains in capital investment and new job opportunities. Between 1945 and 1957, some $1.3 billion was invested and 136,000 new jobs were created. In addition, the federal government spent $1.5 billion to build the Savannah River Plant.[41]

The state's understanding of what was meant by progress and development changed. In 1949, the erection of the eighteen-story Cornell Arms Apartment building in Columbia was hailed as a "landmark and symbol of progress."

When it was completed in 1949, the Cornell Arms Apartment Building in Columbia was "the tallest building between Richmond and Miami." Within a few years capital investment, not the height of a building, would be the barometer of the state's economic development. *Courtesy South Caroliniana Library.*

Eleven years later, the Development Board was trumpeting the statistic that during the 1950s the average annual corporate investment in South Carolina was $117 million.[42] By 1965 the figure had risen to a record $600 million. New highs in capital investment, not skyscrapers, became the yardstick for measuring economic progress.

Town and Country

South Carolina remained a predominantly rural state where, as late as 1960, agriculture was hailed as the basis of the state's economy.[43] But the rural population was declining. In 1940, three out of four Carolinians lived in the country. Twenty years later, only three of five did.[44]

Rural out-migration continued, but at a slower pace than before the war. Instead of the boll weevil and discrimination, it was a combination of federal programs, such as the land bank,

As late as 1960, more than one-half of the state's cotton crop was picked by hand. In 1955, the state Department of Agriculture had touted cotton as "king"; within a year it had been replaced as the leading money crop by tobacco. ***Courtesy South Caroliniana Library.***

and mechanization that reduced the need for farm workers. In 1950, 92 percent of the cotton crop was picked by hand; by 1960, only 51 percent was.[45] Sharecroppers by the thousands lost their jobs—and their homes. Some followed earlier emigrants northward, but a surprising number moved to the state's towns. Yet the 1960 census reported that not a single South Carolina city had 100,000 residents.

Carolinians still thought of themselves as a farming state. As late as 1955, some still thought of agriculture in terms more appropriate to 1855: "*Cotton* . . . is also the King of crops and should anything happen to dethrone this King everybody in America will feel the effects." Within the year, tobacco had displaced cotton as the state's leading money crop.[46]

In many communities, life continued as it had for more than a century. Mules and wagons on the streets of market towns were commonplace. On Saturday afternoon, rural residents continued to gather at country stores or small towns to shop and catch up on the latest news. The state operated canneries in more than one hundred schools, enabling individuals to put up fruits and vegetables safely for winter use. Community life revolved around the local high school where the success of the football team could ease the miseries of a poor cotton crop or a layoff at the mill.

Life in Charleston, Columbia, Florence, Greenville, and other large towns differed only in degree from that in Peak, Pelion, and Prosperity. All of the "big cities" were really just overgrown market and courthouse towns. Rural families shopped there, but they were less likely to arrive in a mule-drawn wagon. There were department stores and small specialty shops instead of general stores. The movie houses had more current features and were more likely to be "air cooled" by the 1950s. In almost all towns, banks closed at noon and shops usually closed Wednesday afternoons. Drive-in restaurants, not infrequently a local version of a Dairy Queen or Atlanta's famed Varsity, became a place for teenagers to hang out after school.

Television came to South Carolina on 19 June 1953 with a broadcast from WCSC in Charleston. Before that, the few individuals who owned oversized Philco or Bendix or RCA sets tried their best to make out the vague, snowy images broadcast from Charlotte's WBTV.

Air-conditioning and television were highly visible signs of the Americanization of South Carolina. The small-town merchant who was afraid that outsiders might make him change his ways was correct. During the 1950s, most Carolinians abandoned midday dinner as the main meal of the day. The leisurely hour-long dinner was replaced by the Yankee custom of bolting down lunch. And, also following northern eating habits, the traditionally light supper became a heavy dinner.

Another cherished tradition that went by the boards during the 1950s was "Big Thursday," the annual football clash between the University of South Carolina and Clemson College. Since the 1890s, this game had been played in Columbia on the Thursday of State Fair Week. This time, the change wasn't perpetrated by any outsiders, but by Clemson officials who decided that they'd prefer to play in Columbia only every other year. On 22 October 1959, forty-six thousand spectators somehow crammed into Carolina Stadium to see the Tigers beat the Gamecocks. In 1960, one of the South's most famous gridiron classics became simply another home and home arrangement.[47]

Air-conditioning, even in businesses, was a rarity until the late 1950s. At home Carolinians still made use of their front-porch rockers. ***Courtesy South Caroliniana Library.***

The Price of Prejudice[48]

It's unlikely that spectators at a "Big Thursday" game realized that some of the state's best professional football prospects were playing for out-of-state colleges or for State College in Orangeburg. Because of segregation, talented young black South Carolina athletes could be found on the rosters of Big Ten, Big Eight, and major independent teams.

In 1945 there was hardly any activity in South Carolina that wasn't segregated. Building upon the Tillman legacy of Jim Crow, later legislatures had decreed that almost every aspect of daily life should be segregated, including such things as separate pay windows, stairs, exits, water fountains, and lavatories. When there were no laws, there were customs. In rural counties, blacks knew to go to town only on Saturdays. In Charleston, black women could push white children in baby carriages around Colonial Lake, but policemen ran off any who pushed their own children in carriages.[49]

Education at all levels was rigidly segregated. In 1945, in an attempt to avert black applications to the state's all white graduate, law, and medical schools, the General Assembly created parallel programs for blacks at Orangeburg. The programs at what became South Carolina State College in 1954 were expensive. The state spent $100 per student semester hour at State College, compared with $17 at the University of South Carolina. Clemson College rejected a $350,000 Atomic Energy Commission grant because the agency required all grant recipients to certify that they barred no person from admission on the basis of race, color, creed, or religion.[50] Blacks were given few educational opportunities; those they were given were grossly inferior. South Carolina had done such a poor job of educating black children that in 1948 it was estimated that 62 percent of the adult black population was either totally or functionally illiterate.[51]

In December 1950, in the Clarendon County town of Summerton, a group of forty black parents filed suit against the local school district. The county's funding of its public schools made a mockery of the doctrine of "separate but equal." There were 6,531 black and 2,375 white students in county schools. In 1951 the county spent $395,329 ($166.45 per student) for whites and $282,950 ($44.32 per student) for blacks. In Clarendon District 22 (Summerton), there were 298 whites and 2,259 blacks. The facilities were so patently unequal that the NAACP had decided to include the Clarendon district in its legal battle to overturn segregation.[52]

The filing of the suit brought an immediate reaction from state officials. Governor James F. Byrnes, shortly after his inauguration in 1951, addressed the General Assembly: "It is our duty to provide for the races substantial equality in school facilities. We should do it because it is right. For me, that is sufficient reason. If any person wants an additional reason, I say it is wise."[53]

The legislators responded to the governor's initiative and passed the state's first sales tax (three cents) to provide increased funding for public education. Between 1951 and 1956, the governor's school program resulted in $124,329,394 being allocated for new construction and buses. About two-thirds of the money went to black schools, although blacks comprised only 40 percent of the school population. In Clarendon District 22, the state spent $894,000 for black school construction and only $103,000 for whites. In some communities, black school facilities were superior to those for whites.[54]

New buildings were only one aspect of what the governor termed his "Educational Revolution." The other major component, school consolidation, reduced the number of school districts from 1,200 to 102. In 1951 there were 82 school districts in Greenville County, 76 in Horry and 51 in Pickens; by 1954, there was only one each in Greenville and Horry counties, while Pickens had two.[55] Antiquated one- and two-room schoolhouses were abandoned and their students moved or "consolidated" in better facilities. Although Byrnes acknowledged that schools were the social and civic centers of many communities, he determinedly pushed consolidation. In only three years, 824 schools were closed.[56] Consolidation also meant that children would be attending school at greater distances from home. In 1951 only 142,00 children rode school buses; by 1955 the number had risen to 241,000.[57]

Taking its lead from the governor, the General Assembly didn't stop with its attempt to provide equal facilities for black and white school children. In 1951 it created a special fifteen-member committee, chaired by Senator Marion Gressette of Calhoun County, to study what would happen if the courts overturned segregation and, if they did, to recommend South Carolina's course of action. The committee, which soon took its chairman's name, was inactive for several years. Over the objections of educators and civic leaders, the legislature placed a referendum on the ballot in November 1952 that called for deleting the constitutional provision requiring the state to maintain public schools. The referendum passed overwhelmingly.

Governor Byrnes, long familiar with the Washington political scene, wasn't willing to let the matter rest. He contacted newly elected President Dwight D. Eisenhower, his political ally, and urged him not to be bound by President Harry Truman's support of desegregation cases. He told the president that segregation was legal and was soundly based on the 1896 *Plessy* v. *Ferguson* decision establishing the doctrine of "separate but equal." Furthermore, the governor advised the president that segregated schools were clearly within the police powers of the state "to promote education and to prevent disorders."[58] All was for naught. On 17 May 1954, the U.S. Supreme Court unanimously ruled that the doctrine of "separate but equal" was unconstitutional. The schools involved in the decision were ordered to desegregate "with all deliberate speed."

South Carolina Reacts to the Brown Decision

Shock. Disbelief. Anger. Hatred. Any of these words could have been used to describe the reaction of most white South Carolinians to the Supreme Court's decision. A group of fifty-two relatively moderate clergy, businessmen, authors, and politicians circulated a petition requesting the General Assembly "interpose the sovereignty of the State of South Carolina between Federal Courts and local school officials."[59] The petition also denounced the "communist influence" apparent in the decision. Within weeks after the decision, white supremacist groups emerged, trying to stir up trouble. The Ku Klux Klan resurfaced but found that it wasn't welcome. State officials considered it a "terrorist" group and newspapers derided Klansmen as "bedsheeters," and "hotheads, crackpots and bullies."[60]

In 1955, when court action to implement the Brown decision began, White Citizens Councils appeared. There was a statewide organization, but the councils were only strong in a few counties. They chose to undermine efforts to desegregate the schools by applying the "squeeze" to those who signed petitions or participated in court cases. The squeeze was not illegal, but it could have a chilling effect on rural blacks. Petitioners might suddenly find that they had no jobs, nowhere to live, and no place to gin their cotton. When whites in Orangeburg applied economic pressure to blacks who had petitioned for desegregation of the city's schools, blacks retaliated. They were supported by a $50,000 boycott fund deposited in Columbia's black-owned Victory Savings Bank. The boycott and counter-boycott dragged on for months before there was an easing of tensions and some compromises were reached.[61]

The 1956 session of the General Assembly was labeled the "Segregation Session" by *News and Courier* reporter W. D. Workman, Jr.[62] A raft of laws was passed, all designed to circumvent the courts and to prevent integration. Edisto State Park was closed. It became illegal for any public employee in South Carolina to belong to the NAACP. Schools and colleges were to be closed rather than desegregated.

Public officials didn't hesitate to say that they'd close schools rather than integrate them. An alarming number of white parents considered segregation more important than education.[63]

However, the Federation of South Carolina Women's Clubs bravely argued against abandoning the public schools,[64] and there were a few individuals who advocated compliance with the Brown decision. Jack O'Dowd, editor of the Florence *Morning News,* reported that "speeches and resolutions against the Supreme Court and the NAACP" had replaced "home, mother, God, and country in South Carolina political circles."[65] His timidly moderate stance was not well received and he was forced to resign. In his farewell editorial, "Retreat from Reason," he restated his position on obeying the law and said that he was not a "pro-integrationist," but an "anti-pro-segregationist."[66] James McBryde Dabbs of Mayesville also advocated compliance. So did Chester C. Travelstead, dean of the University of South Carolina's College of Education. Dabbs was a prophet without honor in his own country. Few of his fellow white Southerners bothered to read *Who Speaks for the South?* Travelstead, at the insistence of powerful political figures, was fired.[67]

The state's politicians behaved exactly as O'Dowd had described. All elected officials, without exception, thundered defiance at the Supreme Court and the federal government. In a record-breaking filibuster lasting twenty-four hours and eighteen minutes, Senator Strom Thurmond tried to block passage of the 1957 Civil Rights Act.

Governor George Bell Timmerman, after seeing to the purge of activists from South Carolina State's faculty, went after faculty at Allen University and Benedict College, two private black institutions in Columbia. He was able to get the State Board of Education to withdraw accreditation for Allen's education program. As a result, black students began applying to the University of South Carolina. The governor's heavy-handed tactics against Benedict only succeeded in rallying the black

Black churches were instrumental in organizing their members to protest segregation. ***Courtesy South Caroliniana Library.***

community and angering conservative Columbia whites who supported the college's administration.[68]

The state's major newspapers continued to assure their readers that most blacks favored the status quo—that if it weren't for "outside agitators" stirring up trouble, all would be peaceful in the Palmetto State. In 1960, when Ernest M. Lander, Jr., a Clemson professor, published a history of contemporary South Carolina, the reviewer in Charleston's *News and Courier* reported that Lander had used the word "Negro"

500 times in 245 pages: "This book seems to lean too heavily on the Negro theme."[69] Lander's book simply attempted to tell the story of South Carolina. The reviewer, like many other South Carolina whites, did not know their state's history and could not understand the social revolution that was overtaking it.

"We Shall Overcome"

If there were one song that became the anthem of the American civil rights movement, it was "We Shall Overcome." Both it and "Eye on the Prize," had their origins on Johns Island.[70] Beginning in the early 1960s, these coastal South Carolina folksongs were heard repeatedly as blacks demonstrated to demand rights that were denied them.

The change in tactics caught whites by surprise, but they had only themselves to blame. Despite court victories, blacks remained second-class citizens in South Carolina. Younger, more vigorous leadership espoused action, not lawsuits.

In January 1960, in the state's first civil rights demonstration, more than 350 blacks marched from Springfield Baptist Church in Greenville to the airport to protest segregated waiting rooms. The next month a group of students from Friendship College in Rock Hill began sit-ins at the lunch counters of Woolworth's and McCrory's. By the summer, demonstrations had spread to Manning, Orangeburg, Denmark, Columbia, Sumter, Charleston, and Spartanburg. Off and on for three years, black protestors took to the streets. They met with limited success.

The Year of Decision: 1963

In looking back over the past thirty years, it is clear that 1963 was a pivotal year in South Carolina history. Just five years earlier, Fritz Hollings had won the governorship by taking a more staunchly segregationist stance ("out-segging") Donald Russell. But the 1960s saw racial turmoil all across the South. Remarkably, South Carolina was relatively peaceful. This was due to the moderation of the state's black and white leadership.

In July 1961, Greenville business executive Charles Daniel astonished an audience at the Hampton Watermelon Festival by telling them that "the desegregation issue cannot continue to be hidden behind the door."[71] He went on to say that South

Carolina should treat its black citizens fairly and provide them with decent educational and employment opportunities. His speech was the first indication that the state's business and political leadership was retreating from its support of segregation.

Six months later, in off-the-record interviews, Governor Hollings urged reporters to have their newspapers prepare the way for the end of segregation. He said flatly that the state's legal defenses would "collapse like a house of cards." *The State* took the lead in reporting the case of Harvey Gantt's application to Clemson and other newspapers followed suit. Behind the scenes, Daniel, Hollings, Senator Edgar Brown, textile lobbyist John Cauthen, Clemson president Robert Edwards, and Greenville *News* editor Wayne Freeman laid the groundwork for Gantt's peaceful admission.[72]

In the fall of 1962 there was violence in Oxford, Mississippi, when the University of Mississippi was integrated. Some legislators urged Governor Hollings to lead a motorcade to Mississippi to show support for Governor Ross Barnett and segregation. He refused and received abusive telegrams.[73] Meanwhile, President Edwards met with Senator Marion Gressette, who was trying to attract a multimillion-dollar corporation to Calhoun County. Edwards was determined to keep Clemson open and to avoid trouble. He was blunt: "Senator, if there's a ruckus at Clemson those people won't even plant scrub oak in Calhoun County."[74] Edwards's stance was

Harvey Gantt registers at Clemson, 28 January 1963. South Carolina's institutions of higher education desegregated peacefully in marked contrast to the violence in other states of the Deep South. *Courtesy* The State.

supported by Daniel and others.

When interviewed by the press about the possibility of Gantt's admission, Senator Brown, who also was a life member of Clemson's Board of Trustees, replied that his position was "that the board of trustees and the administration at Clemson College will not tolerate violence on the Clemson campus."[75] Brown's pronouncement that he stood behind law and order was picked up by the state's press and by the business community. Resolutions supporting Brown's position came from textile executives, the state Chamber of Commerce, the Bankers' Association, and the Broadcasters' Association. Segregationists were caught flat-footed.[76]

On 9 January 1963, Hollings made his farewell speech to the General Assembly: "As we meet, South Carolina is running out of courts. If and when every legal remedy has been exhausted, this General Assembly must make clear South Carolina's choice, a government of laws rather than a government of men. As determined as we are, we of today must realize the lessons of 100 years ago, and move on for the good of South Carolina and our United States. This should be done with dignity. It must be done with law and order."[77]

Shortly thereafter, Governor and Mrs. Donald Russell issued an open invitation "to all the people in South Carolina" to come to a post-inaugural barbecue on the Governor's Mansion grounds. Carolinians, black and white, responded and swarmed the Mansion grounds for the state's first integrated public social gathering since Reconstruction.

The courts ruled on 22 January that Gantt must be admitted to Clemson. In an emotional speech, Senator Gressette told his colleagues: "I have preached peace and good will too long to change my thinking."[78] He then offered to resign as chairman of the Gressette Committee. The senate refused his offer and, instead, gave him a standing ovation. Before the month was over, Gantt had been admitted to Clemson. And, because of careful planning by state officials and their public attitudes, there was no trouble. The *Saturday Evening Post* covered the event with a remarkable story, "Integration With Dignity."

In the state capital, Mayor Lester Bates resolved that Columbia would move toward desegregation rather than be forced by court order to do so. Columbia's business leaders, like their peers across the state, were very image-conscious. They didn't want Columbia to be a Birmingham any more than Senator Brown had wanted Clemson to be an Ole Miss. The mayor gathered together a group of businessmen and presented his idea for desegregating the city. It was a stormy meeting, but out of it came an agreement to drop quietly all racial barriers in public accommodations. The University of South Carolina and the city's schools admitted their first black students. "White Only" and "Colored Only" signs disappeared along Main Street. Desegregation came so quietly and quickly that it had happened before most people realized it. In 1964, *Look* magazine profiled Columbia as one of its "All-American Cities" and praised the city for its moderate racial climate.[79] Other South Carolina cities fell in behind Columbia as segregation of public facilities disappeared.

There was racial peace, but racial progress in other areas was mixed. During the 1960s, almost one-half of all the new manufacturing jobs created went to blacks. The employment of black women in the manufacturing sector increased from 4 percent to 23 percent.[80] But in education, token desegregation was the order of the day. Individual blacks expressed their feelings in a variety of ways. One mother named her son Misterbrown so that whites would have to address him as "Mister." Other blacks gave their dogs names like Malcolm X and Selma.[81]

Despite the undercurrents, South Carolina in 1963 was remarkably different from other Southern states. White South Carolinians rejected mob violence in the 1960s just as they had rejected the Klan in the 1920s. Black Carolinians were moderate in their approach to problems, moderate in the solutions offered, and moderate in the demands made on white Carolinians.[82] Given this relatively peaceful racial climate, the state's white power structure was able to work with the state's black leadership in dismantling segregation.

The Confederate War Centennial

In 1959 the General Assembly created the state's Confederate War Centennial Commission "to commemorate the participation of the State in the Confederate War, 1861–1865."[83] There was an initial flurry of activity and the commission issued several publications encouraging battle reenactments, costume balls, and other public events.

A century after secession, the legacy of the conflict still remained an integral part of state government. In 1956 the Senate had resolved to place the Confederate battle flag behind the rostrum. The Confederate Home for the Widows of Confederate Veterans had been closed in 1957 and its patients placed in private nursing homes. Three of the state's twelve

The South Carolina Confederate War Centennial Commission provided this float to communities wanting to stage parades during the celebration. ***Courtesy South Caroliniana Library.***

legal holidays—Robert E. Lee's Birthday (19 January), Confederate Memorial Day (10 May), and Jefferson Davis's Birthday (3 June)—honored the Lost Cause.

Unfortunately, the observance got off to a rocky start in Charleston. The National Civil War Centennial Commission planned to commemorate the beginning of the war. One of New Jersey's Civil War Centennial Commission members was black. When it was announced that she couldn't stay at the headquarters hotel, the meeting became a mini–civil war. The *New York Times* prophetically observed that the Charleston gathering was "a bad start for a five year observance."[84]

It's clear that the state's Confederate War Centennial Commission envisioned a grand statewide celebration. There were some local celebrations and festivities. Reenactments of the Secession Convention, the firing on Fort Sumter, and the attack on Port Royal were held. Markers were unveiled on the sites of the battles of Aiken and Rivers Bridge. On 2 July 1963, the South Carolina Memorial, a large granite monument honoring the state's Confederate heroes, was dedicated in Gettysburg National Park.[85] Somehow, though, the centennial never really caught on. Perhaps it was the times. Carolinians had other things on their minds. In 1965 a white mill worker dismissed the whole idea: "I don't believe in talking about all this Confederate business—this is America."[86]

The Emergence of Two-Party Politics

Politics, like almost every other aspect of South Carolina society, were altered by events unleashed by the war. The registration of black voters and the national Democratic Party's espousal of equal opportunity gave many Carolina voters pause. In 1936 Governor Olin D. Johnston had delegates to the party's national convention rolling in the aisles as he described the opposition: "There are some grown children down in my state who have never seen a Republican in their lives, and would perhaps run from one if such a strange being wandered too close to their homes."[87] Twenty-six years later, as a U.S. senator, Johnston faced the toughest reelection campaign of his career against Republican W. D. Workman, Jr.

South Carolina's disaffection with The Democracy, as *The State* used to refer to the Democratic Party, began in 1948. The party platform contained a strong civil rights platform which white Southerners considered offensive. They formed the States Rights Party, or Dixiecrats, and nominated South Carolina's governor, Strom Thurmond, for president. Thurmond carried South Carolina and polled more than one million popular votes. The Dixiecrats didn't remain a viable political party after the election, but the number of votes they received indicated white southern voters' discontent with the Democrats.

In 1952 Governor James F. Byrnes, a bitter enemy of Harry Truman and his wing of the party, formed a group called "Democrats for Eisenhower." He invited Ike to Columbia and campaigned for him across the state, but the Democrats carried the state that year and again in 1956.

Throughout the 1950s, all state officials were Democrats. Thurmond, first elected as a write-in candidate in 1954, still considered himself a Democrat. He was unsure as to his reception in Washington after his election, but Lyndon Johnson and the Senate leadership welcomed him, because with his vote they became the majority party.[88]

In the two decades after the war, an increasing number of unhappy South Carolina Democrats joined the fledgling Republican party. One northern Republican party publication

In November, 1947, Governor J. Strom Thurmond wed his secretary Jean Crouch in the Governor's Mansion. *Courtesy South Caroliniana Library.*

In 1952 Governor James F. Byrnes formed "Democrats for Eisenhower" and campaigned with the general in South Carolina. *Courtesy South Caroliniana Library.*

reminded its readers of the roots and traditions of the Grand Old Party and questioned the real Republicanism of the converts. It quoted one South Carolinian on the issue: "There ain't that many Republicans in South Carolina, there's just a lot of mad Democrats,"[89] Perhaps that was true, but the "mad Democrats" voted Republican and that's what counted.

These new Republicans soon outnumbered old-line party members such as civil rights activist I. DeQuincey Newman. Under the leadership of state chairman J. Drake Edens, Jr., the party gradually became a viable entity. The Workman campaign for the Senate in 1962 showed that Republicans could no longer be dismissed lightly. When Senator Thurmond switched parties in 1964, the Republicans were given a tremendous boost. His presence gave the party a visibility and credibility that it had sorely lacked. He campaigned all over the South for Barry Goldwater, the Republican presidential nominee. Goldwater carried South Carolina, the first Republican to do so since 1876.

It was the election of 1966, however, that established the GOP as a true second party. Republicans contested statewide offices, from state superintendent of education to U.S. senator. Thurmond and Second Congressional District Representative Albert Watson were reelected. Party candidates also won six Senate and seventeen House seats in the South Carolina General Assembly.

Some Things Changed; Some Things Didn't

Ben Robertson left his Pickens County home shortly after Pearl Harbor and never returned. Had he lived and returned to South Carolina in 1966, he would have been amazed at some of the changes. The growth of industry would certainly have attracted his attention. So would have the enfranchisement of blacks and the beginnings of the end of segregation. He wouldn't have been happy with the faster pace of life and probably would have wanted to shoot the Columbia businessman who crowed that "Columbia looks as good as Toledo, Ohio."[90]

Robertson would have been horrified at the growth of state government. In 1941 general state appropriations totaled $13,564.99. The General Assembly debated almost every penny of the appropriations bill, from $18.00 for educational equipment for the Citadel's English Department to $24,655.40 for the Confederate Infirmary.[91] The soft-drink tax brought in almost as much revenue as did the state income tax. In 1951 the budget was ten times that of a decade earlier, and in 1966 general state appropriations topped $263,840,205.[92]

There was one thing with which Robertson would have been familiar: the leadership of the General Assembly. Conservative rural legislators such as Edgar Brown and Solomon Blatt of Barnwell County still called the shots. The term "Barnwell Ring" was often bandied about, but most political observers said there was no such thing.[93] When Strom Thurmond ran for governor in 1946, he raised the issue of "the ring" as an attention getter. Donald Russell tried the same thing in 1958 and it was a nonissue.[94]

Blatt and Brown were among the most visible members of the General Assembly. They and like-minded men from small lowcountry counties were reelected repeatedly. Their seniority and experience gave them considerable political clout. As Speaker, Blatt ran the House with an iron hand. He also tested freshmen representatives by giving them difficult assignments to see how they performed. If they met the challenge, then they received plum committee assignments and support in statewide campaigns. If they flubbed their opportunity, they were consigned to the back benches. Future governors

"White Lightnin'" was made in rural areas from the mountains to the sea. This still was seized in the Gumville Section of Berkeley County in 1949. ***Courtesy South Caroliniana Library.***

Religion remained a strong factor in the lives of all South Carolinians. Camp meetings, such as this one at Indianfields Campground near St. George in Dorchester County, continued to be well attended. *Courtesy South Caroliniana Library.*

Hollings and McNair were successful graduates of the speaker's "school."

These politics of friends and neighbors, a very personal sort of politics, survived in South Carolina into the 1960s. Although its roots were in an agricultural past, it served the state well as it tried to cope with the changes ignited by World War II.

South Carolina has changed, but many still cherish and remember the ways of their forebears. In the Charleston Market, a basket weaver continues a centuries-old tradition. *Courtesy* The State (*Doug Gilmore*).

Chapter 4

CHANGES AND CHALLENGES, 1966–1991

> An old South Carolina is dying. A new South Carolina, strong and vital and very proud, is struggling to be born. We will not build the new South Carolina with bricks and mortar. We will build it with minds. The power of knowledge and skills is our hope for survival in this new age.
>
> —Richard Wilson Riley,
> 28 June 1984

In 1983, when Governor Riley made a passionate plea for improving the quality of the state's schools, he also made sure that his listeners understood that times were changing—if, in fact, they had not already changed. The South Carolina society that had emerged from the turbulent Tillman era of the 1890s was gone. The forces unleashed by World War II led to an accelerated pace of change during the 1960s and 1970s. Some changes came about without most Carolinians realizing it; others occurred only after difficult political and social confrontations. Adjusting to these changes and trying to meet the challenges they brought is the story of the past quarter century of South Carolina history.

THE DECLINE OF RURAL SOUTH CAROLINA

The opening essay in the WPA guide to South Carolina asked the question: "Who is the South Carolinian?" The answer was that more than 90 percent of the state's residents had been born here, an overwhelming majority resided in rural areas, and agriculture was the largest sector of the economy. A half century later, the answer was quite different. Between 1960 and 1980, the percentage of South Carolina–born residents declined from eight in ten to seven in ten residents. If historic out-migration patterns had continued, the drop could be easily explained; however, during the 1970s, the century-and-a-half trend of out-migration was reversed. And, for the first time since before 1830, South Carolina's population grew at a faster rate than that of the United States.[1]

The Sun Belt phenomenon was partially responsible for the influx of newcomers, but so was the state's successful selling of itself as a good place in which to live as well as work. Former rural counties such as Beaufort, Berkeley, Dorchester, and Lexington grew rapidly. They also were among those with the largest population of outsiders. By 1980, more than half of the population of Beaufort County and more than 40 percent of the population of Aiken, Berkeley, and Dorchester counties had been born elsewhere. However, in other counties, especially those that remained predominantly rural and agricultural, such as Allendale, Chesterfield, Dillon, and McCormick, the population of native South Carolinians remained above 80 percent.[2]

The state's farm population has continued to decrease with every census. In 1980 only 2 percent of the population (53,000 hardy souls) lived and worked on farms. The decline of the rural population had a devastating effect on small market towns.[3] Carolinians might still live in the country, but they shopped at regional malls that sprang up on the outskirts of larger towns.

Population in what the federal government calls metropolitan statistical areas (MSAs) grew. The same was not true of some of the older central cities that formed the cores of the state's MSAs (Anderson, Charleston, Columbia, Florence, Greenville, and Spartanburg). In 1980 Columbia was still South Carolina's largest city and Charleston was number two. North Charleston, a new city, was close behind its older neighbor, and Greenville dropped to fourth. The old port city was actually smaller in 1980 than it had been in 1940, as residents moved to suburban areas outside the crowded peninsula.[4]

The inner coastal plain and the Pee Dee remained the strongest agricultural sections of the state, but even in those areas, only a small percentage of the population is engaged in farming.[5] Tenant farming and sharecropping virtually disappeared during the 1970s because of mechanization and migration from the farms to the state's cities. In the Pee Dee, bulk metal tobacco barns and mechanical harvesters reduced labor needs by 70 percent.[6]

Not only was cotton no longer king in South Carolina, but it was not even a major crop. In 1945 the state's farmers had planted more than one million acres of cotton. Thirty-five years later, they planted only 97,000. Ironically, the same western states that had destroyed the state's rice industry also played a part in killing off cotton. In Arizona, California, and Texas, mechanized farming on large holdings and modern cotton ginning techniques produced a better grade of cotton more cheaply than did South Carolina's small farms and antique gins.[7]

Soybeans are the most widely planted crop, but livestock provides income for a majority of small farmers. Perhaps one of the most telling illustrations of the changing agricultural scene occurred in 1971 when the commissioner of agriculture made his annual report to the General Assembly. "Consumer Protection," not livestock and crops, was the agricultural service that was highlighted.[8]

As the state became more urbanized, city dwellers became increasingly dissatisfied with state and local governments. Through seniority and constitutionally based apportionment, rural legislators still dominated the General Assembly. Government by county delegation was archaic and unresponsive to the needs of growing communities.

In July 1973, the one hundredth session of the General Assembly adjourned. It was the last one in which individuals

With the mechanization of cotton and tobacco farming in the late 1960s and 1970s, abandoned tenant homes could be seen along most rural roads. *Courtesy South Caroliniana Library.*

Picking peaches is still done mostly by hand, although migrant laborers have mostly replaced local workers. *Courtesy* The State *(Doug Gilmore)*.

were elected to the House of Representatives by counties. The Supreme Court of the United States in *Stevenson* v. *West* ruled that the apportionment of the General Assembly violated the principle of "one man, one vote" and that it must be reapportioned according to population instead of historic political boundaries. Responding to the court's decision, in 1975 the legislature created 124 single-member house districts. Five years later, the Senate was reapportioned into forty-six single-member districts. Single-member districts rendered obsolete traditional county delegation rule. Some smaller counties no longer had a resident senator; a number of house districts crossed county lines.

The Local Government Act of 1975 gave counties some measure of home rule. County councils may enact ordinances, require licenses of various sorts, and raise or lower property tax rates. They have the authority to enact only taxes specifically allowed by the General Assembly. Municipal and county governments must contend with special-purpose districts whose boundaries and functions make little sense. For example, in the Spartanburg County town of Pacolet, eight different "local governments"—Spartanburg County, Spartanburg Soil Conservation District, Spartanburg School District Three, Pacolet Mills Rescue Squad, Pacolet Fire District, Spartanburg Sanitary Sewer District, Spartanburg Waterworks, and the City of Pacolet—determine services. When Hilton Head incorporated as a town in 1983, it could not assume normal municipal service functions, but, instead had to negotiate with six existing special-service districts. Keeping local government fragmented and without real fiscal autonomy is a three-hundred-year-old tradition in South Carolina. Real governmental power remains in the General Assembly.[9]

Single-member districts, however, altered the very nature of the General Assembly. Gone were the power bases that enabled rural legislators to be reelected for decades. In the House, Solomon Blatt of Barnwell County remained a member, but retired as speaker in 1973 after holding that position for more than thirty years. Across the State House lobby, Senator Edgar Brown, also of Barnwell, declined to stand for reelection in 1972.

From the early 1970s until the late 1980s, the character of both houses changed as, one by one, members of the old guard retired or were defeated. Now, in both the House and the Senate, members tend to be more outspoken than in the past. Issues, not seniority or local politics, appear to be more important. And, because of the ever-changing composition of the membership, an individual doesn't have to wait a decade or more before moving into a leadership position.

One of the most negative aspects of single-member districts has been to fragment state government even more. No one is in charge and no one is accountable: not the governor, not the General Assembly, not the judiciary. Without accountability and responsibility, South Carolina state government is ripe for corruption.

"Bubba Gate," Lost Trust and Reform[10]

Since the spring of 1989, South Carolina has been rocked by a series of scandals involving public officials. In May of that year, the president of the University of South Carolina resigned amidst charges that he had misspent university funds. Two months later, the U.S. Attorney for South Carolina announced that a federal grand jury was investigating a number of prominent public officials for allegedly receiving bribes or using drugs. The code name for the government's sting was "Operation Lost Trust." The name for the investigation could not have been more appropriate.

Shortly thereafter, the names of those being investigated were released. Even hardened politicians were stunned. Among the names were seventeen members of the General Assembly (including the speaker pro tempore of the House of

Representatives), a circuit judge, the chairman of the State Development Board, a key aide to the governor, a top Clemson University administrator, six lobbyists, and a Spartanburg businessman.

The initial investigation began with accusations of drug use in the General Assembly and this, in turn, led to a lobbyist's agreeing to go undercover to assist the FBI. Over a period of months, legislators were videotaped accepting cash in exchange for their support of a pari-mutuel betting bill. Some caught in the web turned on their colleagues, and for more than a year South Carolinians wondered "Who's next?"

By October 1991, twenty of those indicted had pleaded guilty, six had been convicted, and one found not guilty, and one still facing trial. The president of the University had also pleaded guilty to using his office for personal financial gain.

The scope of the scandal touched all sections of the state and caused acute embarrassment. The *Economist*, a British publication, ran several articles that could be summed up rather impishly as "corruption in the colonies."[11] The *New York Times* also reported regularly on the ongoing melodrama.[12] Although other states had officials in one sort of difficulty or another, for some reason South Carolina's seemed to capture the most national interest. One Columbian, while traveling in central Florida, was quizzed by a gasoline station attendant about "that mess with your legislature and the university."[13]

Reaction to "Operation Lost Trust" ranged from disgust to calls for a serious look at reforming state government. Beginning with a series of opinion-editorial pieces in August 1990, *The State* newspaper has called for more than reform; it has urged that state government be restructured to more effectively respond to the needs of the state's citizens.[14] The Greenville *News* and the Charleston *News and Courier* have also espoused a major overhaul of state government.

Governor Carroll Campbell ran for reelection in 1990 on a platform calling for reforming state government. So did every other successful statewide candidate from lieutenant governor to state superintendent of education. All campaigned against the outmoded "horse and buggy constitution" forced on South Carolina by Ben Tillman. In January 1991, Governor Campbell appointed a group of thirty-five citizens to a commission to study the restructuring of state government.[15] The South Carolina Commission on Restructuring State Government presented its report to the governor on 19 September 1991. Given the current crisis of confidence in South Carolina government, this effort at reform might have a better chance at success than the twelve studies that have preceded it.[16] Reform may be more likely this time because the state now has a viable two-party system.

Two-Party Politics

Between the end of Reconstruction in 1877 and W. D. Workman, Jr.'s challenge to Olin D. Johnston in 1962, there had been little serious opposition to the Democratic Party. From governor down to county coroner, all elected officials belonged to the party. Republicans were poorly organized and mounted no serious challenges to the Democratic hegemony. Reapportionment of the General Assembly into single-member districts made it easier for Republicans to get elected. Of equal importance in terms of state politics was the registration of more than 220,000 black voters.

The Democratic Party leadership decided in the late 1960s that it would accept blacks as full partners in the political process at all levels. This was a recognition of the political power of the newly registered black voters, most of whom tended to vote for Democrats. The state's delegation to the 1968 Democratic National Convention was racially integrated and it was the only Southern delegation that was not challenged.[17]

In 1970 Herbert U. Fielding of Charleston and James L. Felder and I. S. Leevy Johnson of Columbia became the first black members of the General Assembly since 1900. The Reverend I. DeQuincey Newman became the state's first twentieth-century black senator in 1983. In 1990 there were fifteen black House members and four black senators. All were Democrats. Across the state there were 322 black officeholders, including mayors, city and county council members, and school board members. As more black Democrats seek public office, whites are deserting the party.[18]

Racial identification is something that Republican Party officials have tried to downplay in recent years, but it was not always so. In 1970 Congressman Albert Watson waged the last racially oriented statewide campaign in South Carolina with the full backing not only of the state party but also of the Nixon administration. The tactic backfired. *The State* and other newspapers which normally endorsed Republicans came out for John West, the Democratic nominee. Traditional voting patterns were skewed as suburban Republicans voted for West and moderation.[19]

Four years later, the GOP captured the governorship

when state Senator James B. Edwards defeated Congressman Bryan Dorn. The party also made significant gains in the General Assembly. Edwards left office as one of the most popular elected officials in the state. The decade of the 1980s saw the Republicans increase their strength at all levels. Lexington County became a party stronghold with the most solid bloc of votes of either party. In 1986 the party nominated its "dream ticket" of Carroll Campbell for governor and Tommy Hartnett for lieutenant governor. The election of Campbell and the defeat of Hartnett showed that ticket splitting was still fashionable everywhere except in Lexington County's Republican wards.

Campbell has worked tirelessly to strengthen the party and has used his office effectively. Defections and disunity among Democrats have helped Republicans increase their numbers in the House to forty-one and in the Senate to twelve. There are enough Republicans in the House to uphold a gubernatorial veto, giving the governor a powerful weapon that

James B. Edwards, the first Republican governor in a century, delivers his initial "state of the State" address, 1975. ***Courtesy James B. Edwards.***

he has not shied away from using.

After the filing date closed for the 1990 election, there was considerable amazement among political observers that Republicans had not contested every office in the state. With Senator Thurmond and Governor Campbell at the head of the ticket and a weak Democratic gubernatorial candidate, the party could have conceivably captured control of the General Assembly and dozens of local offices. In statewide races, Republicans ousted incumbent Democrats in races for secretary of state and state superintendent of education. The secretary of agriculture, Les Tindall, switched parties and was reelected only with considerable assistance from Governor Campbell and the Republican establishment.

Since 1968, the future of South Carolina's Republican Party has been linked closely with that of the national party. The state has been a cornerstone of the party's "southern strategy." Thurmond's support of Nixon instead of Reagan for the 1968 nomination and later during the campaign were absolutely crucial in Nixon's winning the White House. During the Nixon, Ford, and Reagan administrations, state party loyalists received federal appointments. Two Carolinians achieved cabinet rank: Fred Dent of Spartanburg, who was Nixon's secretary of commerce, and James B. Edwards, who served as Reagan's secretary of energy. The election of George Bush, engineered in no small part by South Carolinian Lee Atwater, assured state Republicans of another four years of access to the White House.

Not as many South Carolina Democrats have identified

The 1990 election of Republicans Barbara Nielsen as superintendent of education and James Miles as secretary of state and the reelection of Carroll Campbell as governor indicated the GOP's growing popularity. *Courtesy* The State *(Maxie Roberts).*

themselves nearly as closely with their national party. Few statewide officeholders have stumped for their party's presidential nominee since 1960. The 1976 election was an exception, when they campaigned for fellow southerner Jimmy Carter. Carter carried South Carolina in 1976, the only Democrat since John F. Kennedy to do so. The Carter triumph gave South Carolina Democrats the same sort of access that state Republicans enjoyed when their party was in power. Former governor John Carl West as ambassador to Saudi Arabia headed the list of South Carolinians obtaining federal appointments. State party chairman Don Fowler became a key figure on the Democratic National Committee.

After nearly a century of uncontested control of the state, Democrats are facing the possibility of becoming the minority party. The worst fears of white Carolinians a century ago have come to pass: two-party politics, a strong Republican party, and black voters. The realignment of the electorate is just one of the many changes to which South Carolinians have had to reconcile themselves.

"Adjusting to New Circumstances"[20]

South Carolina's previously all-white public colleges had admitted black students in 1963. Desegregation of the state's public schools proceeded more slowly. By 1969, only twelve of ninety-three school districts had permitted small numbers of blacks and whites to attend school together.[21]

Federal officials and federal courts intervened during the 1969–70 school year and ordered school districts in Greenville and Darlington counties totally desegregated in the spring of 1970. Governor McNair, in a desire to head off racial confrontation that had brought violence to other southern communities, appointed fifteen influential citizens to the South Carolina Education Advisory Committee. Chaired by Robert L. Davis, President of the R. L. Bryan Company, the committee worked effectively with business and community leaders in making the transition to unitary schools as peaceful as possible.[22]

State officials did not intervene in either school district's case. When the Supreme Court refused to delay the desegregation order, McNair and the state's business and political leadership urged obedience to the law. The governor, Attorney General Daniel McLeod, and State Superintendent of Education Cyril Busbee met with local school officials to ensure that the desegregation would take place smoothly. McNair went on television in Greenville and Columbia so that he could reach the majority of the students and parents affected by the court order. He emphatically stated that the laws of the land would be enforced. It was a politically courageous position that was unpopular in some quarters. Both Senator Strom Thurmond and Second District Congressman Albert Watson condemned McNair's moderate stance. Watson urged that the state defy the federal government. His posture was quite interesting, because he wanted Democratic officeholders to defy the Republican administration that he had worked so hard to elect.[23]

Segregationists and national news commentators were dumbfounded by the governor's firm statement in Greenville: "I will oppose any attempts to close down public schools. The only way South Carolina is going to continue to grow is through its educational programs." And, regarding potential troublemakers, he said: "A society can't continue to operate

In 1970 Governor Robert E. McNair's courageous stand for obeying the law and keeping open the state's schools led to this cartoon by Eugene Payne. ***Courtesy Robert E. McNair Papers, Institute for Southern Studies.***

without obedience of the law. When we run out of courts and time we must adjust to the circumstances."[24]

Other southern governors still bellowed defiance. In February 1970 Governor John Bell Williams of Mississippi called a meeting of four southern governors in Mobile, Alabama. The governors were determined to devise a strategy to thwart desegregation. McNair was excluded because of his televised statements counseling law and order. As one observer noted: "It was the first time any Deep South governor had spoken out so frankly on the school issue."[25] With defiance and confrontation on their minds, Williams and his fellow segregationists didn't want a moderate in their midst.

In February 1970 the schools in Greenville and Darlington county were totally desegregated. For several weeks, three thousand white students in Darlington boycotted schools. In March a white mob in Lamar overturned a school bus. Federal marshals sat in their cars while highway patrolmen restored order. Later, an all-white jury convicted the bus dumpers.[26]

The remainder of the school year was relatively peaceful, and in a commencement address at the College of Charleston,

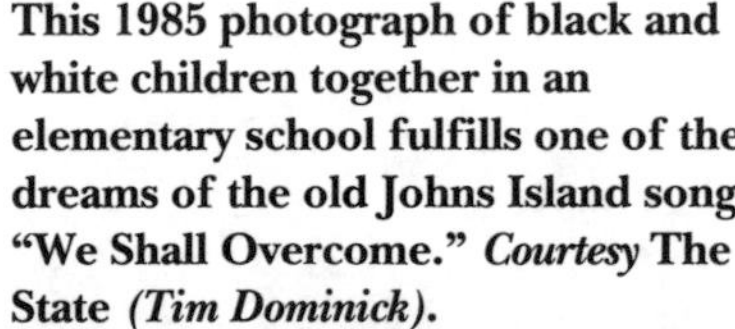
This 1985 photograph of black and white children together in an elementary school fulfills one of the dreams of the old Johns Island song "We Shall Overcome." ***Courtesy*** **The State** ***(Tim Dominick).***

Governor McNair spoke to a wider audience than that on the oak-shaded campus in the port city when he urged his listeners to "steer a course of reason and judgement through the present storms of extremism and polarization."[27] They were words that many would applaud, but some would choose to ignore.

For the fall of 1970, all of the state's school districts were under a federal court order to dismantle their dual school systems and to create unitary systems. Busing was to be used to achieve ideal student body racial mixes reflective of the racial composition of each district. White faculty assigned to previously all-black schools were handpicked in some districts. For example, in Richland District One (Columbia), the district assigned primarily younger teachers with advanced degrees to Booker T. Washington High School. District officials then proudly asserted that the formerly all-black high school had one of the best-educated faculties in the state.

The 1970–71 school year was marred by violence and school closings. Few communities were immune. Armed guards patrolled hallways. Bomb threats occurred with regularity. Individual scuffles turned into racial incidents.

How districts created their unitary system was sometimes a factor in the unrest. In Greenville three black high schools were closed and two others downgraded to junior highs. Blacks felt they'd "had to give up everything they had" in their former schools—mascots, team colors, extracurricular activities.[28] In Spartanburg, where Carver High was merged with Spartanburg High, the students of the merged school chose a new school mascot and new names for the student newspaper and the yearbook.[29] In Orangeburg, Orangeburg and Wilkinson high schools were united as Orangeburg-Wilkinson. And, in Richland District Two, white Dentsville High and black Hanberry High became middle schools and the district built Spring Valley, an entirely new high school. Other districts across the state opted for one or more of these solutions in creating unitary school districts.

Lost, somehow, in all of the desire for proper balances was the impact that unitary schools had on communities, black and white. In Richland One, Olympia High (white) was closed and Webber High (black) became an elementary school. Both schools were more than just high schools; they were community centers as well. Both had proud athletic traditions. They graduated their last classes in June 1970. So did others: Schofield in Aiken, Riverside in Pendleton, Macedonia in Blackville, Haut Gap on Johns Island, Finley in Chester, Gallman in Newberry, Bethune Memorial in Bowman.[30]

Some schools simply did not have the enrollments to justify their existence; others were housed in buildings that should have been closed years earlier. Size or condition meant little to those for whom "their schools" were the heart and soul of their communities. For the second time within a generation, South Carolina's public schools underwent a wrenching realignment. The resulting instability led to the creation of a viable independent school movement.

PRIVATE SCHOOLS

Private education in South Carolina has a long and rich tradition that dates back to the early years of the eighteenth century. A statewide system of public schools is only about a hundred years old. As public education advanced during the first half of the twentieth century, the number of private schools declined.

In 1956 there were only sixteen "private and denominational" schools listed in the state superintendent of education's annual report. Of these, eleven were for whites and five for blacks. Charleston, the site of the state's first modern public schools, had five white private schools. There were three in Columbia and one each in Aiken, Bamberg, and Camden. The black schools were located in Beaufort, Camden, Columbia, Lexington, and Sumter. Total enrollment for all private schools was about eight thousand students. There were more than 563,000 in public schools.[31]

The first private or denominational school to open its doors to students of all races was St. Anne's Roman Catholic School in Rock Hill, which admitted its first black students in 1954.[32] The older, established white private schools such as Heathwood Hall Episcopal School in Columbia enrolled black students in the mid 1960s at about the same time as some of the state's public schools did.[33]

As previously all-white public schools began to admit black students, some white parents sought other educational alternatives. In 1964, with the dropping of the first racial barriers, four private academies were founded. Between 1964 and 1977, nearly two hundred new private or church-related schools came into existence. Under the leadership of Dr. T. E. Wannamaker of Orangeburg and Dr. Charles Aimar of Beaufort, about seventy of the new academies formed the South Carolina Independent School Association (SCISA). In the late 1970s James Henry Hammond Academy in Columbia, with fourteen hundred students, was the association's flagship school.[34]

Private school enrollment peaked at about fifty thousand in 1978. Since then, economic difficulties, declining enrollments, and the gradual improvement of the public school system have taken their toll. Typical of the difficulties facing many of the smaller private schools were those involving Winyah Academy in Georgetown. Winyah closed its doors in July 1986 after a decade of existence. Only 140 students enrolled for the 1985–86 school year and it had needed 200 to remain viable. A $250,000 fund drive had been unsuccessful.[35] Even larger schools have had difficulties.

Another problem facing many members of SCISA was the refusal of the Internal Revenue Service to grant them tax-exempt status because of discriminatory admissions policies. Without IRS approval, contributions to the schools could not be tax deductible. By 1990, many had changed their admissions policies and received tax-exempt status.[36]

Most black private schools disappeared with the advent of integration. One of the last to hold out was Boylan-Haven-Mather Academy in Camden. In 1983 the ninety-six-year-old school closed. Mather, like most of the other black private schools, had been considered elitist by the black community. As one alumnus put it: "Everybody who wanted to be somebody went to Mather."[37] While there might have been an elitist tinge to Mather and other schools like it, they provided for their students a quality education that they could not obtain elsewhere.

Some of the private schools that cropped up in the 1970s have folded, but others have taken their places. Since 1985 there has been an increase in the number of church-related schools. Among these are several elementary schools sponsored by black churches. In the next decade the number of church-related schools is expected to increase.[38] Meanwhile, the older, established independent schools are thriving.

Nonpublic school enrollment has stabilized at about 7 percent of the state's schoolchildren. South Carolinians, for a variety of reasons, are willing to pay for educating their children despite the recent reforms in public education.

Pennies for Education

In 1968 the governor's office commissioned Moody's, a New York investment securities firm, to examine South Carolina's institutions and government. The resulting *Moody Report* was a blueprint for what the state needed to do to improve its services and improve the quality of life of its people. Education was one area the report singled out as a real problem. An unfortunately large number of students were repeating the first grade because they were ill-prepared for even the most basic instruction. And the state ranked forty-ninth in the number of school years completed and the percentage of literate adults.[39] Using the report, Governor Robert E. McNair pushed for a penny increase in the sales tax to fund a statewide kindergarten program. The implementation of a public preschool program helped to prepare children for school.

State funding could only go so far in improving education. Students living in wealthy school districts had distinct advantages over those with small tax bases. It was an unfair system which Governor James B. Edwards resolved to eradicate. In 1977 he appointed a task force to study the problem and make recommendations. The Education Finance Act of 1977 did a great deal to reduce the inequities between rich and poor districts. Under the act, the state provided funds to school districts so that with equal tax effort the State Department's "Defined Minimum Program" would be offered. In essence, the state gives more money to poor districts than it does to affluent ones. The act does not, however, prevent school districts from taxing themselves to provide more than the state-mandated minimum. Consequently, students in some districts enjoy opportunities not afforded others.

The Education Finance Act and two other pieces of legislation, the Basic Skills Assessment Act and the Educator Improvement Act, laid the foundation for what would be the one of the most important pieces of education legislation ever passed in South Carolina. After the spate of legislation in the 1970s, the General Assembly didn't see the need for doing anything else for the state's schools. When Governor Dick Riley first proposed an Education Improvement Act in 1983, he got little support from either legislators or businessmen. In one of the most amazing lobbying efforts in South Carolina history, Governor Riley convinced the business community that without a sound public school system, all of their efforts at development would be for naught. The key to getting businessmen behind the Governor's proposed legislation was the inclusion of provisions for assessing the effectiveness of what was going on in the classroom.

Once Riley had won over the business community, he launched an effective campaign to convince reluctant legislators to pass a penny sales tax increase to improve the state's schools. Parents, teachers, and students joined in the lobbying blitz that refused to let legislators alone unless they agreed to

Governor Dick Riley signs the Education Improvement Act of 1984. In reporting on the effects of the legislation several years later, the *Washington Post* asserted: "No state is more identified with education reform than South Carolina." *Courtesy Richard W. Riley.*

support the bill. The impact of single-member districts with each senator and representative responsible to a particular constituency made this sort of lobbying effort all the more effective.[40]

The Education Improvement Act of 1984 has been hailed in the national media and education circles as a model piece of legislation: "No state is more identified with education reform than South Carolina" *(Washington Post)*; "Once near the bottom, [South Carolina] state schools rank first in improvement" (*Chicago Tribune*); "South Carolina which enacted a one-cent sales tax increase in 1984 to pay for its widely acclaimed Education Improvement Act, stands out as a paragon of reform" (*Wall Street Journal*).[41] The penny sales tax provided 250 million new dollars for education.

During the seven years in which the EIA has been in effect, there have been improvements in some areas. SAT scores have continued to inch up in South Carolina, while nationally they have declined. Student attendance is up and the percentage of high school seniors going to college has increased. Today, roughly 47 percent of the state's high school seniors go on to college. And, more importantly, more of them are staying in college. Teacher salaries are above the southeastern average. Corporations and businesses have taken an active interest in the schools in their communities.

The EIA appears to be working, but there are still problems that have to be resolved. One of the most pressing needs is the replacement of old buildings. Over the course of his eight years in office, Governor Riley visited all ninety-one school districts. He was dismayed to see that a large number of schools dated back to the early 1950s.[42] They had been built with the three-cent sales tax passed during Governor Jimmy Byrnes's administration. Replacing these buildings will be costly.

The crusade to improve education was just one example of the willingness of everyday citizens to get involved in the political process. Until the late 1960s, "getting involved" didn't appear to be acceptable behavior in South Carolina. Ironically, the tactics of those involved in a variety of issues were borrowed from the civil rights movement.

Questioning Plastics in Beaufort—and Development

Since World War II, South Carolina's leaders have actively pursued a policy that embraced industrial development. As one reporter noted: "Probably no other Southern state was quite so evangelistic about industrialization as South Carolina."[43] Therefore, the 1969 announcement that BASF, a German manufacturer, would build a $200 million petrochemical plant in Beaufort County was greeted as another triumph for the state's probusiness posture. The plant was hailed as a boon to one of the most impoverished sections of the state. The director of Penn Center saw BASF as a means by which poor blacks could escape grinding poverty.[44]

South Carolina and BASF officials were unprepared for the furor that followed the announcement of the construction of the plant. Company officials had thought that there would be no problems. After all, a reporter for *The State* had walked into BASF's New York corporate offices and asked: "Now, show me how you aren't going to pollute."[45]

Facing down South Carolina's business and political establishment was an improbable coalition of housewives, professional men, retirees, black fishermen, the Audubon Society,

Friends of the Earth, and Hilton Head developers.[46] Three commercial fishing companies filed suit to stop construction and were joined by three Hilton Head developers. Senator Fritz Hollings allied himself with the opposition and so did Walter Hickel, the secretary of the interior. "A Question of Plastics in Beaufort County" became a national issue.[47]

In March 1970 the company speeded up its construction plans and the plant's opponents became more active. Demonstrators picketed BASF's offices on Hilton Head and the plant construction site. Then, shortly after Representative Alex Sanders of Richland County introduced a bill calling for a moratorium on the plant's construction, BASF gave up. Company officials literally left in the middle of the night.[48]

One Beaufort County politician who had favored the plant was upset. Had BASF come to Beaufort, he said: "We won't be a sleepy village any longer, with a lot of open spaces and untrampled on places. This just has to be. Change is inevitable, you know."[49] Open spaces and clean water were precisely what the unlikely allies in Beaufort County were fighting for. After the BASF fight, a poll of South Carolinians indicated that a majority were concerned about pollution. However, they still wanted development. Those polled thought that state government should be more selective about the types of industries it recruited.[50]

The confrontation in Beaufort between the environment and development was the first of many such battles that would be waged as more and more South Carolinians decided that they did not want to sell their birthright for a mess of pottage—or pollution. When citizens have perceived that the state is not protecting them and their children, they have organized to block new industries or to close down existing ones. The safeguarding of the state's water and air cuts across class, racial, and party lines. Irate citizens have forced plants to close in Lexington and Pickens counties. Carolinians seem more aware of the need to protect the environment. To do so, they are willing to organize, speak out, and, if the situation warrants, be arrested.

Environmentalists and their supporters have made life miserable for politicians and state agencies that fail to safeguard the state's natural resources. In Sumter County, the issue of waste disposal forced a sitting speaker of the house to retire after he was charged with being soft on environmental issues. In 1986 the Legislative Audit Council chastised the Department of Health and Environmental Control for ignoring its own policies on hazardous waste disposal.[51] In 1989

Governor Carroll Campbell surprised legislators when he issued an executive order limiting the amount of out-of-state waste that could be dumped in South Carolina. The General Assembly supported his order with legislation.

Although there has been justifiable concern over the dangers industrial development poses to the environment, it is man that is the biggest polluter of South Carolina. Nowhere is that more evident than along the coast.[52] Overdevelopment is already a reality. Yellow signs warning against shellfishing dot the oyster beds of Murrell's Inlet, once one of the state's richest oyster and clam areas. Water supplies in Horry and Beaufort counties have become more saline as fresh water supplies are drawn down and salt water seeps into aquifers. Large numbers of native Carolinians who once summered in Grand Strand resorts from Garden City to Cherry Grove have abandoned their old haunts to outsiders. Some have sought refuge in the elite enclaves of Debordieu, Hilton Head, and Kiawah; others prefer the "arrogant shabbiness" of Pawley's Island or the down-home feel of Edisto Beach.

In 1988, responding to the need to do something to control untrammelled development, the General Assembly passed the Beachfront Management Act. Uncontrolled development along the coast, spurred by liberal federal flood insurance, had eradicated miles of protective sand dunes and threatened to destroy the beaches that were a mainstay of the state's tourism industry.[53] The primary thrust of the act was that "it is economically unwise and ecologically irresponsible to develop the coast in ways that . . . obliterate storm buffering

Building on the beach can be tricky business. In 1985 unusually high tides reached the foundations of these Fripp Island homes. *Courtesy* The State *(Bill Hornung)*.

Hurricane Hugo leveled the Isle of Palms and other resort communities north of Charleston when it came ashore, 22 September 1989. ***Courtesy*** **The State** ***(Maxie Roberts).***

dunes, and impair the natural processes that create and maintain wide, attractive beaches."[54]

The devastation wrought by Hurricane Hugo in September 1989 underscored the necessity for controlling coastal development. The eye of the category-four hurricane passed twenty miles north of Charleston. A twenty-foot storm surge and sustained winds of 135 miles per hour pounded coastal communities. Destructive winds caused serious damage more than two hundred miles inland. Damage to property and timber exceeded five billion dollars. Thanks to the leadership of Charleston Mayor Joe Riley and Governor Campbell, only seventeen lives were lost and the massive task of rebuilding began immediately.

Déjà Vu With A Difference

The reforms and progress that helped create a new South Carolina came into being against a backdrop of tension and discontent. In 1968 confrontation in Orangeburg between protesting students at South Carolina State College and authorities left three students dead and the state's relatively peaceful race relations strained. Two months later, following the murder of Martin Luther King, Jr., there were riots and disturbances across the state. Curfews were proclaimed in Columbia,

Gaffney, Orangeburg, and in Hampton County.

A series of recent racial incidents have upset the state and tarnished its image. In 1989 an integrated youth group was turned away from a Saluda County pool operated by local Jaycees. A restaurant in Aiken, the Buffalo Room, baldly refused to admit black patrons. And in 1990 an integrated softball team from Fairfield County that entered a charity softball tournament in Norway, South Carolina, was told that no blacks could play on the field.

All of these events triggered immediate responses from government officials and the press. Governor Campbell had the Saluda youth group as his guests at the Governor's Mansion for a cookout and pool party. The attorney general succeeded in having the Buffalo Room's liquor license revoked and the General Assembly in 1990 passed a public accommodations law. In Norway, apologies were issued almost as soon as word of the incident reached the media.

The incidents are disturbing because they recall the late 1960s, when the actions of individuals led to protest and violence. Government officials responded then, but they caught flack from all sides because they insisted on enforcing the law no matter how distasteful that might be to some Carolinians. The response to the recent racial incidents has been encouraging. The public and the state's media have been outraged. That's a healthy and positive sign that changes in law have been accompanied by changes in attitude.

It is ironic that, one hundred years after Ben Tillman began his drive to create a Jim Crow world, the General Assembly of South Carolina enacted legislation forbidding discrimination in public accommodations—and allowing state employees to take a holiday honoring a black civil rights leader.

SOUTH CAROLINIANS ABROAD[55]

Because of the economic, political, and social changes of the last twenty-five years, fewer Carolinians are leaving the state. Some of those who left are returning—especially to retire. This is a welcome trend, but it cannot erase the loss the state has suffered because her sons and daughters had to seek opportunities elsewhere.

The earliest memories that Benjamin Mays of Rambo (Epworth) had was of the Phoenix Race Riots in his native Greenwood County. Mays desperately wanted an education, but until he was seventeen was unable to go to school more than

Nearly one hundred years after Ben Tillman and his allies made the textile mills some of the most segregated places in the state, blacks and whites work side by side. Since the late 1960s, large numbers of black women have moved into the textile work force. *Courtesy* The State *(Gordon Hirsch)*.

four months a year because that was all the schooling Greenwood County provided for black children. He attended the preparatory school at State College, where he "came to the conclusion that I could never do what I hoped to do or be what I aspired to be if I remained in the state of my birth. I had to seek a new world." After college in the North, Mays returned briefly to teach at State College, but left after he married. In 1940 he began a twenty-seven-year tenure as president of Morehouse College in Atlanta. Among his many students was Martin Luther King, Jr. In July 1980, the General Assembly of South Carolina honored its distinguished native son by hanging his portrait in the State House.[56] He was the second black Carolinian so honored.

The first black Carolinian (and the first woman) to have her portrait in the State House was Mayesville native Mary McLeod Bethune. Like Mays, Bethune left South Carolina for better educational opportunities. In 1904 she founded what would become Bethune-Cookman College in Daytona Beach, Florida, and for thirty-eight years she served as its president. In

1935 President Franklin D. Roosevelt appointed her to the Advisory Board of the National Youth Administration and within a year she had become the Director of its Negro Division.[57]

Mays and Bethune are still household names in South Carolina. Less well known today, but just as important in the field of education, are Benjamin Brawley and Kelly Miller. Miller, a native of Winnsboro, was the son of a free man of color and a slave woman. In order to obtain the education he craved, he, too, left South Carolina, but he never lost his affection for the Palmetto State.[58] A multitalented individual, Miller was a mathematician, historian, sociologist, newspaper columnist, and dean of arts and sciences at Howard University. He was a pioneering sociologist who wrote widely and forthrightly about race relations in the United States.[59] In *Race Adjustment: Essays on the Negro in America,* Miller made reference to two South Carolina incidents: the murder of a black postmaster in Lake City and the appointment of William D. Crum as collector of customs in Charleston. His description of Charleston could just as easily have been written by someone in the Poetry Society two decades later: "The good old city had sunken into its traditional ways, reveling in the glory of by-gone days, dreaming of things of yore in the shadow of Calhoun's monument, and basking in the soft, silvery moonlight over the Battery."[60]

Benjamin Brawley, a Columbia native, wrote about the port city in a similar vein. He described Charleston as "An old woman with silken hair, in lavender and old lace, opening a book at a pressed rose."[61] Like Mays, Bethune, and Miller, Brawley left South Carolina to obtain his education. An English professor, Brawley was the author of twenty-six books, including a biography of Paul Dunbar.[62] In 1934 a group of young black women in Columbia formed the Brawley Book Club.[63]

White and black Carolinians were fans of the music of Camden native Brook Benton ("The Boll Weevil Song" and "Rainy Night in Georgia") and Trio native Chubby Checker ("The Twist"). Jazz great Dizzy Gillespie hails from Cheraw. In 1976 Gillespie addressed a joint session of the General Assembly. Four years later, while in Columbia to receive an honorary degree from the University of South Carolina, he was an honored guest at the Governor's Mansion.[64]

Heavyweight champ "Smokin' Joe" Frazier was born in Laurel Bay in Beaufort County. After winning the heavyweight title in 1968, he returned to Beaufort County where he purchased Brewton Plantation, once the property of one of colonial South Carolina's largest slave merchants. In 1970, in an address to the General Assembly, he commented that when he left the state in 1960 there had been few opportunities for young blacks and now he could look out and see black faces in the State House chamber.[65]

It was not segregation, but a search for greater opportunities, that caused Stanley Donen, Carlisle Floyd, and Jasper Johns to leave South Carolina. In 1940 Donen left Columbia and went to New York where he landed a part in *Pal Joey*, starring Gene Kelly. He and Kelly became fast friends and Donen's career prospered. In Hollywood, he choreographed several films and then moved on to directing them. Although he has directed films of all types, he is known primarily for his musicals, such as *Singing in the Rain, Seven Brides for Seven Brothers,* and *Funny Face.*[66] Carlisle Floyd of Latta was the son of a Methodist clergyman. South Carolina Methodists move their clergy every few years, so Floyd grew up in McClellanville, Bethune, Jordan, and North. After taking courses at Converse College, he studied at Syracuse. In 1956 his opera *Susannah* had its New York premiere and is today the most frequently performed American opera. Jasper Johns, "the venerated father of the Pop Art movement of the '60's," was the son of a failed cotton farmer. His family life was unsettled and he lived with a variety of relatives in Allendale, Columbia, and Sumter. He spent a year and a half at the University of South Carolina where he studied art with Catharine Rembert. After a stint in the army, he settled in New York in 1953. In 1958 he had his famous one-man show at Leo Castelli's Gallery. Among the paintings exhibited there were "Flags" and "Target With Four Faces." Currently his paintings bring some of the highest prices for a living American artist.[67]

All of these "South Carolinians Abroad" made their reputations outside their native state. What is interesting is their continued ties with South Carolina. Mays and Bethune returned here on a number of occasions to work with black youth. Miller and Brawley studied and understood South Carolina history and included numerous references to their home state in their writings. Frazier and Johns have homes here—Frazier in Beaufort and Johns at Edisto Beach. The music of Benton and Checker draws on their rural South Carolina background. One of Floyd's operas, *The Passion of Jonathan Wade,* is set in Reconstruction Columbia. Floyd and Donen have named the South Caroliniana Library as the depository for their papers.

Apparently, it's hard to get South Carolina out of your system. In a campaign address at an Easley Kiwanis Club prayer breakfast, Greenville native Jesse Jackson said: "My family has our American roots in Pickens County."[68] In March 1988 Jackson won 53 percent of South Carolina votes cast in the Democratic primary and a majority of the state's delegates to the party's national convention.[69] Ben Tillman probably is still spinning in his grave.

South Carolina Then and Now

The South Carolina of today is very different from the South Carolina of the 1890s. To Ben Tillman, the world would appear to be upside-down. Two-party politics; white Republicans; black Democrats. A strong statewide public school system open to all; coeducation at Clemson and Winthrop; a thriving, nine-campus University of South Carolina. A real state museum; flourishing county museums in places like St. Matthews and Lexington; a "furrin" cultural

In 1969 civil rights leader I. DeQuincey Newman led Senator Ernest F. Hollings on a fact-finding tour of the state's poverty areas. The highly publicized tour was an indication of how much the social and political climate of South Carolina had changed. *Courtesy South Caroliniana Library.*

festival, Spoleto. Liquor by the drink and hordes of tourists. Community-sponsored Fourth of July celebrations. Only fifty-three thousand farmers and "King" egg, tobacco, soybean, peach, or cow—depending on the county. Interstate highways and air-conditioning. Lengthy legislative sessions dominated by lawyer-legislators. A state agency actually recruiting out-of-state industries. The purchase of locally owned businesses by outside interests, including his old enemy, *The State*, by Knight-Ridder.

Families and friends welcome home the 413th Chemical Company (120th Army Reserve Command) of Florence, which spent seven months in Saudi Arabia. The unit was one of many South Carolina reserve and National Guard units activated during operations Desert Shield and Desert Storm. ***Courtesy 120th Army Reserve Command.***

When Union Camp Corporation decided to build a multimillion-dollar paper mill, it also decided to spend one million dollars to restore historic Kensington Plantation. The old and the new South Carolina coexist peacefully in lower Richland County. ***Courtesy Union Camp Corporation.***

It's a new South Carolina in 1991, the product of one hundred years of change. As the state looks forward to the twenty-first century, its citizens are better prepared than were their great-grandparents in 1891. Yet, like their forebears, they know that they are the products of their heritage—and most especially of the legacy of the last hundred years.

A South Carolina Chronology, 1890–1991

1890	The 1890 census reveals that South Carolina's population is 59.9 percent black. Proportionally, there are more black Carolinians in 1890 than there had been on the eve of the Civil War.
3 November 1890	Benjamin Ryan Tillman of Edgefield County and his populist supporters easily defeat the aristocratic old guard in what Tillman terms "The Revolution of 1890."
18 February 1891	The first issue of *The State* newspaper appears in Columbia. Founded initially as a partisan anti-Tillman paper, it would soon become one of the most powerful and influential newspapers in South Carolina.
3 March 1891	Civil War hero Wade Hampton III retires from the U.S. Senate after having been turned out of office by the Tillman-dominated legislature.
8 November 1892	South Carolina voters shun the Populist ticket and support Grover Cleveland's winning effort.
24 December 1892	Tillman coerces the General Assembly into creating a state liquor monopoly, the Dispensary.
1 May 1893	The World's Columbian Exposition opens in Chicago. Special excursion trains carry South Carolinians to the fair. Eight years later, South Carolinians would have their own grand exposition in Charleston.
6 June 1893	Clemson College, now the state's Morrill Land Grant school, opens its doors.
27–29 August 1893	A killer hurricane strikes the coast south of Charleston. More than two thousand residents are killed. Winds do considerable damage as far inland as Columbia.
1894	The Panic of 1893 hits South Carolina. Cotton prices drop to 4.6 cents a pound. On the best farmlands in the state, it costs farmers six to eight cents a pound to plant cotton.
30 March 1894	Riots erupt in Darlington when Dispensary officials run amuck and rough up the local citizenry. Fanned by press reports in *The State* and the *News and Courier*, South Carolina briefly teeters on the brink of civil disorder before Governor Tillman finds enough militia units that will obey him and restore order.

6 November 1894	George Washington Rembert, the state's only remaining black Congressman, is elected to his last term in the House of Representatives.
4 March 1895	Tillman enters the U.S. Senate.
15 October 1895	Winthrop College, a state normal school for white women, opens its doors in Rock Hill.
4 December 1895	After meeting in Columbia for two months, delegates to the state's constitutional convention adopt a new constitution to replace the Reconstruction Constitution of 1868. Dominated by Tillman and his followers, the convention effectively eliminates meaningful black participation in the political process and creates a cumbersome, fragmented system of government that still plagues South Carolina today.
3 March 1896	The General Assembly establishes the Colored Normal, Agricultural, and Industrial College in Orangeburg. When it opens in the fall of 1896, this school is the only state-supported institution of higher education for black South Carolinians.
28 May 1896	The U.S. Supreme Court hands down its decision in *Plessy* v. *Ferguson*, in which it establishes the doctrine of "separate but equal."
13 November 1896	The University of South Carolina wins the first "Big Thursday" football contest with upstate rival Clemson, 12–6.
8 November 1898	On election day in Greenwood County, a bloody race riot erupts in the Phoenix Community.
29 September 1900	Four days of racial rioting in Georgetown end the racial accommodation of the "fusion" plan by which the county's offices had been divided between white Democrats and mostly black Republicans. The plan had been in effect since the end of Reconstruction.
1 December 1901	The Interstate and West Indian Exposition, one of Charleston's few attempts at New South boosterism, opens with much fanfare.
15 January 1903	Lieutenant Governor James Tillman, nephew of Senator Tillman, shoots and kills N. G. Gonzales, the editor of *The State*, within the shadow of the State House. Tillman's murder trial is moved to Lexington County where a jury acquits him.
17 February 1906	For the third time in its hundred-year history, the South Carolina College is rechartered as the University of South Carolina.
16 February 1907	The General Assembly abolishes the Dispensary, long a source of corruption and controversy.
1907	Carrier installs the first commercially successful air-conditioning units.

12 July 1908	The battleship *South Carolina* is launched at Philadelphia. She is the first of the "dreadnaughts" with revolving turret guns. The eight-million-dollar ship represents "the greatest change in warship design since the Civil War."
3 November 1908	Ellison D. "Cotton Ed" Smith wins the first of six elections to the United States Senate.
8 November 1910	Woodrow Wilson is elected governor of New Jersey. The election attracts a great deal of attention in South Carolina because Wilson spent his formative teenage years in Columbia. With numerous kin still living in the capital city, Wilson is considered by many to be a "local boy."
8 November 1910	Coleman Livingston Blease, the hero of the state's millworkers and sharecroppers, is elected governor.
27–28 August 1911	A fierce hurricane makes landfall south of Charleston and destroys the rice crop. The storm ends the commercial growing of rice in South Carolina.
7 November 1911	John P. Grace, a Roman Catholic Irishman, hands Charleston's old guard a shocking defeat when he wins the mayor's office.
5 November 1912	Woodrow Wilson is elected president. South Carolinians are ecstatic.
3 November 1914	The election of Richard I. Manning as governor indicates that South Carolinians are willing to participate fully in the Progressive Era.
8 February 1915	*Birth of a Nation,* set in Reconstruction-era South Carolina, premieres.
21 October 1915	*Birth of a Nation* premieres in South Carolina.
29 February 1916	The General Assembly passes a child labor law that raises the minimum age for employment from twelve to fourteen.
March 1916	The United States experiences border problems with Mexico. Among the troops sent to deal with Pancho Villa are several units from South Carolina.
1917	The boll weevil enters South Carolina. Alice R. H. Smith and D. E. H. Smith publish *The Dwelling Houses of Charleston,* a pioneering work of historic preservation.
May 1917	*The Crisis,* the magazine of the National Association for the Advancement of Colored People, reports thirteen new chapters in southern cities, among them Charleston and Columbia.
18 May 1917	Congress passes the Selective Service Act. During the course of World War I 307,350 South Carolinians register; 54,284 are drafted.

4 March 1918	Camden native Bernard Baruch is named to head the War Industries Board.
September 1918	The Spanish Influenza epidemic hits South Carolina. In four months more than 170,000 cases and 7,400 deaths are reported.
1919	The boll weevil destroys the sea island cotton crop. Another staple disappears from the South Carolina economy.
1920	Cotton prices drop from 40 cents a pound to 13.5 cents. Farmers lose $140 million even before harvest. This is the beginning of the agricultural depression in South Carolina.
21 April 1920	Susan Frost convenes a group of Charleston community leaders for the organizational meeting of the Society for the Preservation of Old Dwellings.
26 August 1920	The Nineteenth Amendment to the Constitution, giving women the right to vote, is ratified—but not by South Carolina.
March 1921	In Columbia, the Palmetto State Festival (called Palmafesta), a South Carolina version of Mardi Gras, is celebrated as part of the effort to attract tourists.
October 1921	The Poetry Society of South Carolina publishes its first *Yearbook.*
1922	For the first time since 1820, South Carolina whites outnumber blacks. "Carolina in the Morning" is a national hit.
2 June 1923	Governor Thomas G. McLeod declares a day of fasting and prayer for the deliverance of the cotton crop threatened by drought and the boll weevil.
21 March 1924	The General Assembly passes the "6-0-1" Act, providing significant funding for public schools.
15 June 1924	American Indians become U.S. citizens.
1925	South Carolina leads the nation in the production of cotton textiles.
10–21 July 1925	The Scopes Trial occurs in Dayton, Tennessee. Scopes is convicted and it remains illegal to teach evolution in the state of Tennessee.
29 December 1925	Trinity College in North Carolina becomes Duke University under the terms of James B. Duke's will. South Carolina's Furman University in Greenville is also a major beneficiary of Duke's benevolence.
17 May 1926	John T. Woodside, a Greenville industrialist, begins to develop Myrtle Beach as a major resort.

19 February 1927	Governor John G. Richards launches a crusade to enforce the state's blue laws.
19 April 1927	The South Carolina House of Representatives kills a bill outlawing the teaching of evolution in the state's colleges and public schools.
1928	"Carolina Moon," another romantic song about the state, makes it big.
6 November 1928	Mary Gordon Ellis of Jasper County is elected to the South Carolina Senate—the first woman ever elected to the General Assembly.
1929	The General Assembly investigates unrest in the textile industry and supports workers' claims of mistreatment by management.
14 May 1929	Julia Peterkin of Fort Motte wins the Pulitzer Prize for *Scarlet Sister Mary,* a novel about black Carolinians.
24 October 1929	On Big Thursday at the State Fairgrounds in Columbia, Clemson rallies to defeat the University of South Carolina. On Wall Street, it is Black Thursday.
1930	The Great Depression ravages the state's already depressed agricultural sector. Sixty percent of the state's farmers are tenants; 30,000 of 188,000 farms are abandoned, as twenty-four of forty-six counties lose population.
9 May 1930	The state's first radio station, WCSC in Charleston, begins broadcasting. Two months later, WIS goes on the air in Columbia.
4 November 1930	James F. Byrnes defeats incumbent Senator Coleman L. Blease.
September 1931	Panic grips the nation as a four-month run on banks begins. More than eight hundred banks close their doors.
13 October 1931	In reaction to mindless progress and the continued purchasing of architectural features from its old buildings, Charleston City Council passes a Historic Preservation Ordinance, the nation's first.
31 December 1931	The People's State Bank, with forty-four branches across the state, fails.
June 1932	Cotton prices drop to 4.6 cents a pound, the lowest level since 1894.
8 November 1932	Franklin D. Roosevelt receives his greatest margin of victory (98 percent) in South Carolina.
31 March 1933	The Civilian Conservation Corps is established. In South Carolina, the CCC's activities result in a system of state parks.

April 1933	In anticipation of the passage of the Agricultural Adjustment Act, South Carolina farmers begin plowing up 500,000 acres of newly-planted cotton.
12 May 1933	The Agricultural Adjustment Act passes. Congressman Hampton P. Fulmer of Orangeburg is a key figure in maneuvering this legislation through the House of Representatives.
18 May 1933	The Tennessee Valley Authority is created. Congressman John J. McSwain of Greenville is the co-author of the bill.
August 1933	Twenty-five percent of the state's population is on relief.
1934	Janet Gaynor and Robert Young star in "Carolina," a Hollywood romance set on an antebellum South Carolina plantation.
19 May 1934	Legislation creating the South Carolina Public Service Authority (Santee Cooper) passes.
1 September 1934	More than one million textile workers across the nation begin a month-long textile strike. In South Carolina 45,000 workers walk out, and in Honea Path seven strikers are killed.
1935	The last two volumes of David Duncan Wallace's *History of South Carolina* are published in New York by the American Historical Society.
1 August 1935	A National Advisory Board for the National Youth Administration is appointed. Among its members is Mayesville native and noted educator, Mary McLeod Bethune. Within a year Bethune is named director of the NYA's Negro Division.
28 October 1935	Governor Olin D. Johnston declares the South Carolina Highway Department to be in rebellion and mobilizes the National Guard to keep his opponents out of their offices.
25 June 1936	Senator "Cotton Ed" Smith walks out of the Democratic National Convention in Philadelphia to protest an invocation by a black clergyman. *Time* magazine labels the senator "a conscientious objector to the twentieth century."
24 February 1937	The first annual meeting of the South Caroliniana Society is held in Columbia. The society, dedicated to collecting and preserving manuscript materials, soon helps the University of South Carolina's library and manuscript holdings rival those of the venerable South Carolina Historical Society.
11 August 1938	FDR stops in Greenville enroute to Washington and appears to support Olin D. Johnston against "Cotton Ed" Smith in a heated U.S. Senate race. The strategy backfires as the state's voters resent the president's meddling in local affairs. They give Smith one last term.

8 November 1938	Charleston's charismatic mayor, Burnet Maybank, is elected governor. He is the first Charlestonian to win the State House since the Civil War.
28 January 1939	The Riviera Theater opens in Charleston. The art deco movie palace seats 1,193 and is "air cooled" by giant fans blowing over blocks of ice.
18 April 1939	Land clearing begins for the massive Santee Cooper project. In less than three years, in February 1942, Santee Cooper is generating electricity.
17 March 1941	The National Gallery of Art opens in Washington. York native David Edward Finley is its first director. Eight years later in October 1949, Finley is the founder and first president of the National Trust for Historic Preservation.
February 1942	Twenty-four B-25 crews stationed at the Columbia Army Air Base, in response to a call from General Jimmy Doolittle, volunteer for a secret mission.
5 March 1942	The General Assembly creates the South Carolina Ports Authority to develop the ports of Beaufort, Charleston, and Georgetown.
18 April 1942	General Doolittle leads a squadron of B-25s in a raid on Tokyo.
27 May 1943	President Roosevelt names James F. Byrnes Director of War Mobilization. The nation's press soon calls the South Carolinian the "assistant president."
14 April 1944	The General Assembly, in a frantic attempt to negate the Supreme Court's outlawing of the all-white Democratic primary, passes a record 147 pieces of legislation in six days. The South Carolina Democratic Party is now a private club.
19–20 July 1944	At the Democratic National Convention, Byrnes expects to be the party's vice presidential nominee. FDR instructs his lieutenants to "clear it with Sidney" [Hillman], a labor leader. Labor and black leaders oppose Byrnes and Truman gets the nomination instead.
1945	A price index of food stuffs, maintained by the South Carolina Department of Agriculture, reports that food prices have risen 66 percent since 1941.
16 February 1947	A Greenville mob lynches Willie Earle, a young black man. The state prosecutes the suspects and the June trial becomes a media event. The Earle case closes a dark chapter in South Carolina history. It is the state's last lynching.
23 June 1947	The Taft-Hartley Act, limiting labor's gains during the New Deal, is passed. It will be seven years before South Carolina becomes a "right to work" state.

12 July 1947	Judge Waties Waring of Charleston stuns the state by declaring the legislature's efforts to maintain the all-white primary to be invalid.
17 July 1948	Meeting in Birmingham, dissident southern Democrats nominate South Carolina's Governor J. Strom Thurmond for president.
2 November 1948	Truman wins! The president receives 304 electoral votes to 189 for Thomas Dewey, his Republican challenger. Thurmond garners 38.
15 April 1949	The General Assembly ratifies a voter-approved amendment to the state constitution that legalizes divorce.
28 November 1950	The U.S. Atomic Energy Commission announces that a new production facility will be built on a 250,000-acre site in Aiken and Barnwell counties. A number of small communities, including the town of Ellenton, will have to be razed.
December 1950	Charging that Clarendon County's segregated schools discriminated against their children, forty black parents file a lawsuit. As it moves through the courts, the case is joined with other segregation cases in *Brown* v. *Board of Education.*
19 April 1951	Governor James F. Byrnes's proposal for a three-cent sales tax to improve public education in South Carolina becomes law. School consolidation is also part of the plan and more than 1,200 school districts are reduced to 102.
4 November 1952	Governor Byrnes leads a "Democrats for Eisenhower" movement that produces 158,000 votes for the general. Enough voters, however, remain loyal to the Democrats to carry the state for Adlai Stevenson.
19 June 1953	The state's first television station, WCSC in Charleston, goes on the air.
19 March 1954	South Carolina becomes a "right to work" state and outlaws the closed shop.
20 March 1954	The modern State Development Board is created and immediately begins a series of aggressive campaigns designed to lure industries to South Carolina.
17 May 1954	The United States Supreme Court hands down its decision in *Brown* v. *Board of Education.* "Separate but equal" is no longer the law of the land.
2 November 1954	Flouting the state's political hierarchy, Strom Thurmond wins a write-in candidacy for the Senate seat left vacant by the death of Burnet Maybank. This is the only time in American history that a U.S. senator has been elected by a write-in ballot.
1955	The South Carolina Department of Agriculture proclaims that "Cotton is King" still. Within a year, tobacco replaces cotton as the state's leading agricultural crop.

8 March 1956	The General Assembly passes the Hart-Arthur Act requiring stores selling Japanese textiles to display a large sign: "Japanese Textiles Sold Here." The act creates something of an international brouhaha. The situation eventually calms down after the Japanese voluntarily curtail their textile exports to the United States.
1 July 1957	The Confederate Home is closed.
January 1958	Sumter High School graduate Jasper Johns has a spectacular one-man show at Leo Castelli's Gallery in New York. This is the beginning of the Pop Art movement.
25 February 1959	The General Assembly establishes the Confederate War Centennial Commission.
22 October 1959	The last Big Thursday is held at the State Fair.
1 January 1960	In Greenville, black South Carolinians march from the Springfield Baptist Church to the airport to protest segregated waiting rooms. This is the first civil rights demonstration in the state.
2 February 1960	In neighboring North Carolina, students at North Carolina A & T College in Greensboro stage the first sit-in. Within weeks sit-ins are occurring all over South Carolina and the South.
15 May 1961	The state begins its widely-acclaimed and much-imitated technical education program.
1 October 1962	James Meredith enrolls at the University of Mississippi and racial violence erupts. With Meredith's enrollment, South Carolina remains the only Southern state whose public institutions of higher education remain segregated.
6 November 1962	Republican candidate William D. Workman, Jr., wages a savvy campaign against incumbent U.S. Senator Olin D. Johnston. Workman loses, but his candidacy clearly shows that the South Carolina Republican Party is now a force in state politics.
9 January 1963	On the eve of desegregation at Clemson, outgoing Governor Ernest F. Hollings addresses the General Assembly and urges all South Carolinians to "remember the lessons of one hundred years ago" and "move on for the good of South Carolina and our United States."
16 January 1963	Newly inaugurated Governor and Mrs. Donald S. Russell host a barbecue on the grounds of the Governor's Mansion for "all South Carolinians." It is the first racially integrated state function in nearly a century.
28 January 1963	Segregation barriers fall in higher education as Harvey Gantt is admitted peacefully to Clemson. In marked contrast to the violence at Ole Miss, the *Saturday Evening Post* features a story on South Carolina entitled "Integration With Dignity."

2 July 1964	President Lyndon Johnson signs the Civil Rights Act into law.
16 September 1964	Senator Strom Thurmond announces that he is switching from the Democratic to the Republican Party.
29 October 1964	South Carolina's Charles Townes wins the Nobel Prize in Physics.
3 November 1964	Republican presidential candidate Barry Goldwater with Thurmond's full support carries South Carolina. Not since Rutherford B. Hayes in 1876 has a Republican presidential candidate won in the Palmetto State.
6 August 1965	The Voting Rights Act becomes law. South Carolina is one of the states affected by the new legislation. More than 220,000 black Carolinians register to vote.
8 November 1966	Robert Evander McNair is reelected governor without opposition in either the primary or general election. His election is a confirmation that South Carolina has opted for racial moderation and progress.
20 June 1967	In response to pressures from the state's tourist industry, the "brown bag" law enabling individuals to carry their own liquor into restaurants is passed.
8 February 1968	A confrontation between students at South Carolina State College and state law enforcement officials leaves three young black men dead. Orangeburg is a shock to a state that has prided itself on racial accommodation.
4 March 1968	Beaufort native Joe Frazier wins the World Heavyweight boxing title in New York City.
1 August 1968	Under the provision of the Housing and Urban Development Act of 1968 (and subsequent amendments), federal flood insurance will cover buildings along the country's coasts. This act is a boon for developers and South Carolina's resorts.
5 November 1968	Richard M. Nixon's "southern strategy" wins him the election. Senator Strom Thurmond plays a key role in developing the strategy and subsequent presidential campaign.
31 January 1969	Senator Ernest Hollings begins his much-publicized "Hunger Tour" that reaches a national audience. The tour draws mixed reactions in South Carolina.
27 January 1970	Governor Robert E. McNair goes on television and vows that South Carolina's public schools will remain open—and desegregated.

25 June 1970	The Charleston production of *Porgy and Bess* is the highlight of the yearlong Tricentennial Celebration of South Carolina's founding. This is the first South Carolina performance ever of George Gershwin's opera based on DuBose Heyward's novel, *Porgy*.
August–September 1970	Under federal court order, the state's public schools open under a unitary school plan.
3 November 1970	Representatives James L. Felder and I. S. Leevy Johnson of Richland County and Herbert U. Fielding of Charleston County are the first black Carolinians elected to the General Assembly in the twentieth century.
28 June 1972	At the end of the Ninety-ninth General Assembly, veteran State Senator Edgar Brown of Barnwell County announces that he will not stand for reelection. As speaker pro-tempore of the Senate and chairman of the Finance Committee, Brown has been one of the most powerful individuals in the state.
25 June 1973	The U.S. Supreme Court rules in the case of *Stevenson* v. *West* that South Carolina must reapportion its House of Representatives into single-member districts.
6 July 1973	The One Hundredth General Assembly adjourns. It is the last assembly with "at large" county delegations.
31 July 1973	Solomon Blatt of Barnwell County resigns as speaker of the house after holding the position longer than any other individual in the history of the General Assembly.
5 November 1974	James B. Edwards is the first Republican elected to the South Carolina governorship since 1874.
25 June 1975	The Local Government Act becomes law, giving the state's counties a measure of home rule.
4 July 1976	A magnificent ceremony in Columbia's Trinity Episcopal Cathedral is one of many South Carolina celebrations in honor of the Bicentennial of the American Revolution.
2 November 1976	Jimmy Carter wins South Carolina as the Democrats mount an effective southern strategy of their own.
10 June 1977	At Governor Edwards's urging, the General Assembly passes the Education Finance Act that redistributes state tax dollars to poorer school districts.

28 March 1979	A breakdown in the cooling system of a nuclear reactor at Three Mile Island, Pennsylvania, results in a major nuclear accident.
30 July 1979	In response to Three Mile Island, South Carolina creates a Nuclear Advisory Council and curtails the shipment of low-level nuclear waste into the state.
19 November 1979	Camden native Lane Kirkland is elected the second president of the AFL-CIO.
1980	The agricultural census reveals that there are only 53,000 bona fide farmers in the state and that only 97,000 acres of cotton were planted in the previous year.
28 October 1980	The Catawba Indians file a suit in Rock Hill laying claim to 140,000 acres of York and Lancaster counties.
4 November 1980	Ronald Reagan sweeps South Carolina and reaffirms the tendency of the state's voters to be "presidential Republicans"; the state's voters approve a constitutional amendment permitting the governor to serve a second consecutive term.
April 1981	South Carolinians react with a mixture of embarrassment and amusement as Rita Jenrette, the estranged wife of former Congressman John Jenrette, titillates the nation with a "bares all" story in *Playboy*.
12 April 1981	The space shuttle *Columbia* is launched from Cape Canaveral. Representatives of the state's capital city are on hand for the occasion.
1 January 1982	Clemson University defeats Nebraska in the Orange Bowl and wins the national championship.
2 February 1983	Columbia native Joseph Bernardin becomes a prince of the Roman Catholic Church in a ceremony at St. Peter's in Rome. As archbishop of Chicago, Cardinal Bernardin is one of the country's most influential religious leaders.
25 October 1983	The Reverend I. DeQuincy Newman, longtime civil rights leader, wins a special election in Richland County for a seat in the South Carolina Senate. He is the first black senator in the twentieth century.
28 May 1984	Memorial Day is observed as a state holiday for the first time in South Carolina. Prior to this, the state, like most southern states, did not recognize Memorial Day because of its associations with the Union victory in 1865.
28 June 1984	The Education Improvement Act, a much-heralded reform of the state's public schools, is signed by Governor Richard W. Riley.

11 December 1984	Congress passes the Gramm-Rudman-Hollings Act which mandates a balanced federal budget by 1991. Senator Ernest F. Hollings, long a critic of Congressional spending, is instrumental in the bill's becoming a law.
28 January 1986	The space shuttle *Challenger* explodes after liftoff. Lake City native Ron McNair is one of the astronauts killed.
28 October 1986	The State-Record Company of Columbia announces its sale to the Knight-Ridder newspaper chain.
19 March 1987	Evangelist Jim Bakker resigns from his ministry in York County. This is the beginning of the downfall of his religious empire that includes Heritage USA and the PTL Club.
11 September 1987	Pope John Paul II visits Columbia.
5 March 1988	George Bush trounces his opponents in the South Carolina Republican Primary.
8 March 1988	With the momentum generated by his South Carolina victory, Bush sweeps the southern primaries on "Super Tuesday." Columbia native Lee Atwater is the architect of Bush's successful drive for the nomination and the election campaign that follows.
7 June 1988	Responding to the dangers posed by overdevelopment of the Carolina coast, the General Assembly passes the Beachfront Management Act.
22 September 1989	Hurricane Hugo, a dangerous category-four storm, makes landfall just north of Charleston about midnight. With 135-mile-per-hour winds that do not dissipate readily, the storm cuts a swath through the state that leaves 17 dead, 64,000 homeless, 270,000 jobless, and damage in excess of five billion dollars. Twenty-two of the state's forty-six counties are declared disaster areas.
18 July 1990	The U.S. Attorney for South Carolina announces that the FBI has seized the records of a number of legislators. This is the beginning of the unfolding of Operation Lost Trust, a political scandal of major proportions.
24 August 1990	The first South Carolina reserve units are activated in support of Operation Desert Shield. Before the conflict in the Middle East is over, more than six thousand South Carolina reserve and National Guard personnel are called up.
6 March 1991	Governor Carroll Campbell appoints the South Carolina Commission on Government Restructuring, a citizen's panel, to make recommendations for the overhaul of the state's outmoded and fragmented government.

24 April 1991	In a White House Rose Garden Ceremony, President Bush posthumously awards the Congressional Medal of Honor to Corporal Freddie Stowers of Sandy Springs for valor during World War I. Stowers thereby becomes the only black American to win the nation's highest award in either world war.
24 June 1991	South Carolina National Bank, the state's largest, announces that it will merge with Wachovia Bank and Trust Company of Winston-Salem, North Carolina. SCN is the last of the state's major independent banks. The merger marks the end of a century of South Carolina's efforts to create its own capital base.
3 July 1991	A giant military parade in Columbia is one of the highlights of Freedom Week, a celebration in honor of Operation Desert Shield/Desert Storm.
19 September 1991	The Commission on Government Restructuring presents its findings to the governor. The 350-page report calls for major reorganization and streamlining of South Carolina government. If implemented, the plan will eliminate the last vestiges of Ben Tillman's "Revolution of 1890."

Notes

Preface

1. John Andrew Rice, who grew up in South Carolina before World War I, entitled his memoirs *I Came Out of the Eighteenth Century* (New York, 1942). Rice was a keen observer and the evidence is overwhelming that in many ways South Carolina began this century one hundred years behind most of the rest of the country.

2. Kelly Miller, "These 'Colored' United States: South Carolina," *Messenger*, December 1925, p. 376.

3. Benjamin Brawley, "The Southern Tradition," *North American Review*, 226 (1928): 309.

4. When the General Assembly created a commission to coordinate the state's celebration of the one hundredth anniversary of the American Civil War, they used the term *Confederate War.* Inez Watson, ed., *Legislative Manual*, 1960, p. 265.

5. "Committed to Bull Street" is a longtime South Carolina euphemism for being sent to the State Mental Hospital, which for more than 150 years has been located on Bull Street in Columbia. This is the phrase that a Carolinian in 1960 would have used.

Chapter 1—A Political Bull Ring, 1891–1916

1. Francis Butler Simkins, *Pitchfork Ben Tillman: South Carolinian* (Baton Rouge, 1944), p. 154.

2. Peter A. Coclanis, *The Shadow of a Dream: Economic Life and Death in the South Carolina Lowcountry, 1670–1920* (New York, 1989), pp. 128–29. Coclanis and Lacy K. Ford, "The South Carolina Economy Reconstructed and Reconsidered: Structure, Output, and Performance, 1670–1985," in Winifred B. Moore, Jr., Joseph F. Tripp, and Lyon G. Tyler, Jr., eds., *Developing Dixie: Modernization in a Traditional Society* (New York, 1988), p. 102.

3. Wallace, 3:337.

4. David L. Carlton, *Mill and Town in South Carolina, 1880–1920* (Baton Rouge, 1982), pp. 18–19.

5. In 1890 South Carolina produced 747,190 bales of cotton as compared to 353,412 in 1860. U.S. Department of the Interior, Census Office, *Abstract of the Eleventh Census: 1890* (Washington, 1894), p. 91. William J. Cooper, Jr., *The Conservative Regime: South Carolina, 1876–1890* (Baltimore, 1968), pp. 134–42.

6. Cooper, pp. 126–27, 129.

7. *Abstract of the Eleventh Census*, pp. 46–47.

8. Wallace, 3:386.

9. Coclanis, p. 142.

10. Wallace, 3:322–25.

11. Simkins, p. 154. Wallace, 3:344–45, 351.

12. Simkins, pp. 72–81.

13. Cooper, p. 189.

14. Cooper, pp. 205–06. Simkins, pp. 70–81. Wallace, 3:340, 344–45.

15. Simkins, pp. 158–61.Wallace, 3:337, 151.

16. Daniel W. Hollis, *University of South Carolina, Vol. 2: From College to University* (Columbia, 1956), pp. 126–29, 133–34, 148. Lewis P. Jones, *South Carolina: One of the Fifty States* (Orangeburg, SC, 1985), p. 600. Simkins, pp. 153–43, 161.

17. Jones, *Stormy Petrel: N. G. Gonzales and His State* (Columbia, 1973), p. 137. Samuel L. Latimer, Jr., *The Story of "The State," 1890–1969, and the Gonzales Brothers* (Columbia, 1970), pp. 9–17.

18. Wallace, 3:354–55.

19. Jones, *Stormy Petrel*, pp. 207–09. Wallace, 3:358–59, 375.

20. Julian J. Petty, *The Growth and Distribution of Population in South Carolina: Bulletin #11, Prepared for South Carolina State Planning Board* (Columbia, 1943), p. 64.

21. George B. Tindall, *South Carolina Negroes, 1877–1900* (Columbia, 1952), pp. 58–63.

22. Tindall, p. 73.

23. Asa H. Gordon, *Sketches of Negro Life and History in South Carolina* (2nd. ed., Columbia, 1971), pp. 65–68. Tindall, p. 83.

24. Tindall, p. 87.

25. Tindall, pp. 119–20.

26. Tindall, p. 216.

27. C. Vann Woodward, *The Strange Career of Jim Crow* (2nd. rev. ed., New York, 1966), pp. 50–51.

28. Woodward, *The Strange Career of Jim Crow,* pp. 50-51.

29. For examples of Jim Crow customs, see Mamie Garvin Fields with Karen Fields, *Lemon Swamp and Other Places: A South Carolina Memoir* (New York, 1983), pp. 10, 46–50, 55, 64–65.

30. Rice, p. 42. In his memoirs Rice says this incident occurred in 1892, but he describes segregated waiting rooms which didn't exist until after 1896, and Columbia's new Union Station wasn't built until 1902.

31. Gordon, pp. 146–47. Idus A. Newby, *Black Carolinians: A History of Blacks in South Carolina from 1895 to 1968* (Columbia, 1973), pp. 133–34.

32. Simkins, p. 218.

33. Tindall. p. 303.

34. Carlton, *Mill and Town,* pp. 115–16, 244–45.

35. Carlton, *Mill and Town,* pp. 40–41.

36. Carlton, *Mill and Town,* p. 40.

37. Carlton, *Mill and Town,* pp. 60–63.

38. Walter B. Edgar, ed., *South Carolina: The WPA Guide to the Palmetto State* (Columbia, 1988), p. 4. DuBose Heyward, *Mamba's Daughters* (New York, 1929), p. 43. Carlton, *Mill and Town,* pp. 83–87.

39. Grace Lumpkin, *The Wedding* (reprint ed., Carbondale, IL 1976), p. 188.

40. Carlton, *Mill and Town,* pp. 43, 48–49.

41. Ben Robertson, *Red Hills and Cotton: An Upcountry Memory* (1942; paperback ed., Columbia, 1973), pp. 95–96, 274–78. Carlton, *Mill and Town,* pp. 5, 8, 11, 76, 133.

42. Carlton, *Mill and Town,* 69. Robertson, pp. 274–77.

43. Carlton, *Mill and Town,* p. 133.

44. Carlton, *Mill and Town,* p. 135.

45. Carlton, *Mill and Town,* pp. 161–62.

46. Carlton, *Mill and Town,* pp. 154–55.

47. Wallace, 3:425–27.

48. Carlton, *Mill and Town,* pp. 224–25.

49. In 1910 Blease won the governorship by 5,645 votes; of these 3,565 came from Charleston, where his opponent garnered only 820. Wallace, 3:426.

50. Carlton, *Mill and Town,* pp. 235–39.

51. Wallace, 3:429.

52. Carlton, *Mill and Town,* pp. 215–17.

53. Carlton, *Mill and Town,* p. 11.

54. Carlton, *Mill and Town,* p. 181. John Joseph Duffy, "Charleston Politics in the Progressive Era" (Ph.D. dissertation, University of South Carolina, 1963), pp. 1–2. Woodward, *The Origins of the New South* (Baton Rouge, 1967), pp. 371–73.

55. Carlton, *Mill and Town,* pp. 36–37.

56. Fields, pp. 4, 13. Gordon, pp. 94–99. Newby, pp. 103–05. Tindall, pp. 224–27.

57. *Abstract of the Eleventh Census,* pp. 228–29, 232–33. U.S. Department of Commerce and Labor, Bureau of Census, *Thirteenth Census of the United States Taken in the Year 1910: Abstracts of the Census* (Washington, 1913), pp. 227–28. William H. Hand, "The Sad State of the High Schools in 1910," in Ernest F. Lander, Jr., and Robert K. Ackerman, *Perspectives in South Carolina History: The First 300 Years* (Columbia, 1973), p. 313.

58. Carlton, *Mill and Town,* pp. 174–78, 234–35.

59. U.S. Census Office, *Abstract of the Twelfth Census of the United States, 1900* (Washington, 1900), pp. 70–71, 73.

60. Hollis, *University,* pp. 177, 267, 269, 270. Lander, *A History of South Carolina, 1865–1960* (Columbia, 1970), p. 142.

61. Duffy, pp. 47–53.

62. Lawrence H. Larsen, *The Rise of the Urban South* (Lexington, KY, 1985), p. 118.

63. Carlton, *Mill and Town,* p. 155.

64. U.S. House of Representatives, *The Miscellaneous Documents of the House of Representatives for the First Session of the Fifty-Second Congress: Volume 50, part 18. Eleventh Census of the United States 1890: Vital and Social Statistics, Part III: Statistics of Death* (Washington, 1896), pp. 338–45.

65. Carlton, *Mill and Town*, pp. 169–70.

66. Carlton, *Mill and Town*, pp. 169–70.

67. Jones, *Stormy Petrel*, pp., 157, 250, 282.

68. Wallace, 3:407.

69. Duffy, p. 25.

70. Tindall, p. 236.

71. Don Barton, *The Clemson-Carolina Game, 1896–1966* (Columbia, 1967), pp. 30–31. Hollis, *University*, 227–28. Lander, p. 148.

72. Tindall, pp. 239, 249, 252, 257–58. Wallace, 3:400n.

73. Carlton, *Mill and Town*, p. 246.

74. Lander, pp. 53–55. Wallace, 3:439–41.

75. Robert M. Burts, *Richard Irvine Manning and the Progressive Movement in South Carolina* (Columbia, 1974), pp. 91–93. Wallace, 3:441.

76. Mrs. John Van Vorst and Marie Van Vorst, *The Woman Who Toils: Being the Experiences of Two Ladies as Factory Girls* (New York, 1903), pp. 223–24.

77. Carlton, *Mill and Town*, pp. 194–95, 244–48.

78. Carlton, *Mill and Town*, pp. 226–27.

79. Duffy, pp. 210–11.

80. William Augustus Shealy to Patterson Wardlaw, *A Columbia Reader* (Columbia, 1986), pp. 117–18. Carlton, *Mill and Town*, p. 228.

Chapter 2—A Land of Monuments and Memories, 1916–1941

1. "A Place of Promise," *New York Times*, 26 December 1930, p. 12. A year later the *New York Times* once again used the same tone in an article on Charleston, "An Old City that Lives on as a Monument," *New York Times Magazine*, 1 November 1931, p. 21.

2. "The New Era Edition," *The State* (Columbia), 18 December 1930. This special 124-page edition celebrated the completion of the Lake Murray dam and what plentiful electric power would do for South Carolina. Some six thousand extra copies were printed and mailed across the country.

3. Wallace, 3:434, 438, 444, 456–57.

4. Wallace, 3:445–47.

5. Wallace, 3:447.

6. Wallace, 3:449.

7. Newby, pp. 188–89.

8. Wallace, 3:456.

9. John Hammond Moore, "Charleston in World War I," *South Carolina Historical Magazine*, 86:41–42.

10. The 30th (Old Hickory) Division and the 371st Regiment of the 93rd (Negro) Division saw action along the Hindenberg Line near Bellincourt, France. Wallace, 3:454. Wallace incorrectly has the 371st Regiment assigned to the 92nd Division, but current Department of the Army records indicate the 93rd. "WWI Vet Gets Overdue Medal," *Soldiers*, June 1991, p. 3.

The states whose citizens received the most Medals of Honor were in order: New York (10), Illinois (8), South Carolina (7), New Jersey (7), California (6), Missouri (6), and Tennessee (6). The state's seventh Medal of Honor winner, Corporal Freddie Stowers, a farm worker from Sandy Springs, received his award posthumously in 1991. In a ceremony in the East Room of the White House, President George Bush presented the medal to Stowers's sisters. The corporal from Sandy Springs was the first black American to receive the Medal of Honor in either World War I or World War II. On 28 September 1918, Stowers was mortally wounded while leading his company in a charge against a German position. He was a member of Company C, 371st Regiment. *The State*, 24 April 1991, p. 1B.

11. Mary Katherine Davis Cann, "The Morning After: South Carolina in the Jazz Age" (Ph.D. dissertation, University of South Carolina, 1984), pp. 11–14. Jones, *South Carolina: A Synoptic History for Laymen* (rev. ed., Orangeburg, SC., 1978), p. 244.

12. Edgar, ed., *South Carolina*, pp. 60, 64. Wallace, 3:478.

13. Jack Irby Hayes, Jr., "South Carolina and the New Deal, 1932–1938" (Ph.D. dissertation, University of South Carolina, 1972), pp. 408–10. *South Carolina: Economic and Social Conditions* (Columbia, 1945), p. 135.

14. M. K. D. Cann, p. 51. Robertson, p. 164.

15. M. K. D. Cann, pp. 8–9, 54, 66–67. Hayes, p. 410.

16. "Those were the draining years on the cotton farms—the 1920s. Nearly all of the strongest tenant families left the cotton fields." Robertson, p. 278.

17. Edgar, ed., *South Carolina*, p. 61. Jones, *Synoptic History*, p. 244.

18. Edgar, ed., *South Carolina*, p. 60. Lander, pp. 120–21. Wallace, 3:447.

19. In 1930 South Carolina still had only 1.5 hospital beds per 1000 people. This was one-half the national average and the lowest ratio in the country except for Mississippi. Nineteen of the state's forty-six counties did not even have a hospital. Wallace, 3:475–76.

In 1940 there was only one physician per 1,507 South Carolinians, as compared to the national average of one per 798; and there was only one dentist per 5,307 as compared to the national average of one per 1,728. Petty, *Growth*, p. 132.

One-third of all children born were delivered without a physician present. The death rate for white mothers in childbirth was 7.7 per 1000; for black mothers it was 81.8. *South Carolina: Economic and Social Conditions*, p. 215. Between 1919 and 1929, approximately one infant out of ten died at birth. Edward H. Beardsley, *A History of Neglect: Health Care for Blacks and Mill Workers in the Twentieth-Century South* (Knoxville, 1987), p. 17.

With hard times came poor nutrition and disease. Malaria deaths rose from 279 in 1931 to 450 in 1937. Pellagra deaths more than doubled from 306 in 1920 to 811 in 1930. Women and children were hit particularly hard. South Carolina, Board of Health, *61st Annual Report* (1940), p. 98. Beardsley, pp. 54, 56–57. Wallace, 3:477–78.

20. M. K. D. Cann, p. 25. Jones, *South Carolina*, p. 618. Lander, pp. 117, 120–21. Wallace, 3:479.

21. M. K. D. Cann, p. 16.

22. M. K. D. Cann, p. 68. Hayes, p. 4. Robertson, p. 278.

23. Petty, *Growth*, pp. 99–100.

24. Newby, pp. 200–01.

25. M. K. D. Cann, pp. 71–73.

26. Edgar, *History of Santee Cooper, 1934–1984* (Columbia, 1984), p. 4.

27. Petty, *Growth*, pp. 32, 35. Petty, *Twentieth Century Changes in South Carolina Population: A Study Prepared for the State Organization for Associated Research* (Columbia, 1962), p. 160.

Most South Carolinians migrated northward; there were, however, a number who migrated to Georgia and Florida. A smaller number went west. The northern migration was predominantly black and the southern and western migrations predominantly white. Petty, *Twentieth Century Changes*, p. 180.

28. Petty, *Growth*, pp. 156–60, 168. *South Carolina Economic and Social Conditions*, pp. 35–37.

29. M. K. D. Cann, pp. 80, 94, 101. Edgar, ed., *South Carolina*, p. 70. Wallace, 3:481.

30. M. K. D. Cann, pp. 138–39.

31. M. K. D. Cann, pp. 102–03, 140, 150.

32. M. K. D. Cann, p. 157. Jones, *Synoptic History*, p. 256.

33. M. K. D. Cann, pp. 110, 112, 114–15. One of the tragic results of the low wages was a decline in the health of mill operatives and their families. A poor diet—primarily of fatback, cornmeal, and molasses—often led to pellagra. Women and children seemed to be particularly susceptible. Beardsley, pp. 54, 57.

34. M. K. D. Cann, p. 21. Wallace, 3:458.

35. M. K. D. Cann, p. 181.

36. Hayes, pp. 4, 152. Jones, *South Carolina*, p. 640. Wallace, 3:479.

37. M. K. D. Cann, pp. 164–70.

38. Wallace, 3:462, 474.

39. M. K. D. Cann, pp. 274–76, 279–80.

40. Jones, *Synoptic History*, p. 250. Wallace, 3:483.

41. M. K. D. Cann, p. 291. Before the 1920s the state had not made the funding of education a priority. In 1919 Governor Manning noted that the amount of money "given by the people of South Carolina for humanitarian and relief purposes during the War is almost four times the amount appropriated for educational purposes by the State during the past four years." "Governor Manning's Report on His Administration, 1919," in Elmer D. Johnson and Kathleen Lewis Sloan, *South Carolina: A Documentary Profile of the Palmetto State* (Columbia, 1971), pp. 546–49.

42. M. K. D. Cann, pp. 291–95. Edgar, ed., *South Carolina*, pp. 3, 95. Lander, p. 123. For many years South Carolina had the highest illiteracy rate in the country. In the 1930s, one excuse for the tremendous number of black illiterates was that the "smartest" ones had migrated. Those who remained in the state were "shiftless." No mention was made of the state's refusal to spend as much money for black schools as it did for whites. Sadly, this argument was still being circulated half a century later. V. S. Naipaul, "A Reporter at Large: The

Religion of the Past," *New Yorker*, 24 October 1988, p. 94. Edgar, ed., *South Carolina*, p. 54.

43. M. K. D. Cann, pp. 406–08.

44. Lander, p. 130.

45. Carlton, "Unbalanced Growth and Industrialization: The Case of South Carolina," in Moore, Tripp, and Tyler, eds., p. 121.

46. Lander, p. 103.

47. W. B. Rast to Lewis O. Rast, 3 December 1912. Lewis O. Rast Papers, a private collection, Swansea, SC.

48. Paul S. Lofton, "A Social and Economic History of Columbia, South Carolina During the Great Depression, 1929–1940" (Ph.D. dissertation, University of Texas-Austin, 1977), p. 166. Jones, *Synoptic History*, p. 249. Lander, pp. 102–05.

49. Wallace, 3:467–68.

50. Coclanis, p. 156.

51. M. K. D. Cann, pp. 191, 404–05. Ludwig Lewisohn, "South Carolina: A Lingering Fragrance of the Past," *Nation*, CXV (1922): 36–38.

52. The year 1926 was a banner one for coastal developers. Charters were issued for Ocean Drive on 5 April, Edisto Beach on 24 April, Floral Beach (Garden City) on 26 April, Myrtle Beach on 17 May, and Sea Island Homes of Beaufort on 9 June. Charter numbers 14706, 14733, 14737, 14774, 14807. South Carolina, Secretary of State. Records, Secretary of State: Charter Private Companies, 14200–14999. South Carolina Department of Archives and History. M. K. D. Cann, p. 435. South Carolina's beaches, like all public accommodations, were segregated. Atlantic Beach, "the black pearl of the Grand Strand," was developed by black Carolinians for black vacationers.

53. M. K. D. Cann, p. 427.

54. Marion Lucas, *Sherman and the Burning of Columbia* (Lexington, KY, 1976), p. 128.

55. See the "Cities and Towns" and "Tours" sections of Edgar, ed., *South Carolina*, pp. 157–468.

56. Fields, pp. xvii–xxiii. Robertson, pp. 3–5.

57. Fields, p. xviii. On 28 March 1936, an editorial in *The Palmetto Leader*, a black newspaper in Columbia, commented on the capital city's sesquicentennial celebration: "Columbia's 150th Anniversary," *A Columbia Reader*, p. 122.

58. Robertson, p. 295.

59. Robertson, pp. 92, 119, 202.

60. Tindall, p. 287.

61. Miller, "These 'Colored' United States," p. 377, 400.

62. Lewisohn, p. 36.

63. Edgar, ed., *South Carolina*, p. 3.

64. Robertson, pp. 3–5. For generations, South Carolinians and Virginians have referred to North Carolina as the valley of humiliation between two mountains of pride.

65. M. K. D. Cann, pp. 1, 212.

66. Newby, p. 225.

67. M. K. D. Cann, p. 1. Jones, *Synoptic History*, p. 247.

68. Robertson, pp. 26–27. Jones, "Address, Fiftieth Anniversary Meeting," University South Caroliniana Society *Program of the Fifty-first Meeting* (1987) p. 6.

69. Rutledge, p. 128.

70. Charles B. Hosmer, Jr., *Preservation Comes of Age: From Williamsburg to the National Trust, 1926–1949*, 2 vols. (Charlottesville, 1981), 1:234–37, 240.

71. M. K. D. Cann, p. 3.

72. Barbara Bellows, "At Peace With the Past: Charleston, 1900–1950," in Lynn Robertson Myers, ed., *Mirror of Time: Elizabeth O'Neill Verner's Charleston* (Columbia, 1983), pp. 1–5.

73. M. K. D. Cann, p. 206. Edgar, ed., *South Carolina*, p. 122. Allen University Quartet Suggested Melodies, "Hand Me Down De Silver Trumpet" (Chicago, 1923).

74. Lewisohn, p. 36.

75. J. H. Easterby, *Guide to the Study and Reading of South Carolina History* (Columbia, 1950) is the most complete bibliography of nonfiction works published during this period.

76. See Easterby. Virtually every major commercial press of the 1920s and 1930s is listed. Southern university presses, especially the University of North Carolina, also appear frequently in the *Guide*.

77. M. K. D. Cann, p. 204.

78. M. K. D. Cann, pp. 207–10.

79. Bellows, p. 5.

80. In the 1930s the Right Reverend Kirkman Finlay, first bishop of the Episcopal Diocese of

Upper South Carolina, wrote: "Yet when our country went to war, the Negro was called to the Colors, and expected to contribute to every drive for money. They, for whom their country did so little, were expected to be just as patriotic as we who received its every benefit. Nobly they responded too.

"How long will they continue to suffer in patience and silence? How long will they continue to sing: `My Country 'tis of thee, sweet land of liberty'—for the white man." Kirkman G. Finlay, *A Collection of Sermons, Notes, and Clippings*, ed., Augustus T. Graydon (Columbia, 1965), p. 82.

81. M. K. D. Cann, p. 258.

82. Newby, p. 234.

83. Finlay, pp. 75–91.

84. Tindall, p. 66.

85. Newby, p. 232.

86. Newby, p. 233.

87. James Francis Cooke, "Ol' Car'lina" (Philadelphia, 1920), one of many tunes published in the North during the 1920s and 1930s that portrayed a romantic, stereotypically "Ole South," South Carolina.

88. Charles F. Kovacik, "South Carolina Rice Coast Landscape Changes," in *Proceedings: Tall Timbers Ecology and Management Conference #16* (Thomasville, GA, 1982), p. 56.

89. Lewisohn, p. 38.

90. Edward D. C. Campbell, "The Celluloid South: The Image of the Old South in American Film, 1903–1978" (Ph.D. dissertation, University of South Carolina, 1979), p. 121.

91. Campbell, 119.

92. Fant H. Thornley to E. T. H. Shaffer, 11 October 1941, Thornley Papers, South Caroliniana Library, Columbia, South Carolina.

93. Sidney Holden and Roy Reber, "Charleston Cabin" (New York, 1924). Gus Kahn and Walter Donaldson, "Carolina in the Morning" (New York, 1922). Billy James, "Carolina Sweetheart Waltz" (New York, 1925), Benny Davis and Joe Burke, "Carolina Moon" (New York, 1928). Sonny Skyler, Bette Cannon, and Arthur Shaftel, "Just a Little Bit South of North Carolina" (New York, 1941).

94. Newby, pp. 194–95. Holden and Reber, "Charleston Cabin."

95. Paul Wesley, "Moonbeams on the Strand" (Murrell's Inlet, SC, 1926). Gene Halsey and Holmes Haselden, "The Azalea Waltz" (Charleston, 1935). The illustration on the latter sheet music features an antebellum beau and belle surrounded by azaleas.

96. Edgar, ed., *South Carolina*, p. x.

97. Edgar, ed., *South Carolina*, pp. 3–7. Robertson, pp. 82, 100.

98. Robertson, pp. 98–99, 105.

99. Wallace, 3:492. Edgar, ed., *South Carolina*, p. 6.

100. Robertson, pp. 95–96.

101. Rutledge, p. 47.

102. Robertson, p. 290.

103. M. K. D. Cann, pp. 429–30.

104. Kovacik, "Rice Coast Landscape Changes," pp. 57–58. Kovacik, "Hunting Plantations in Lowcountry South Carolina," a paper delivered at the Association of American Geographers, April 1988, pp. 6, 8.

105. Heyward, p. 31.

106. M. K. D. Cann, p. 365.

107. M. K. D. Cann, p. 365.

108. M. K. D. Cann, pp. 366–68.

109. Hayes, p. 26. Edgar, ed., *South Carolina*, p. 43.

110. M. K. D. Cann, pp. 374–77. Wallace, 3:465.

111. M. K. D. Cann, pp. 361–62.

112. M. K. D. Cann, pp. 337–40, 354. Hollis, *University*, p. 316. Lander, p. 159.

113. U.S. Department of Commerce and Labor, Bureau of Census, *Special Reports; Religious Bodies: 1906; Party I: Summary and General Tables* (Washington, 1910), pp. 264–67. M. K. D. Cann, pp. 339–40. Lander, pp. 162–63. Edgar, ed., *South Carolina*, p. 103.

114. Jones, *Synoptic History*, p. 252.

115. M. K. D. Cann, pp. 350–51.

116. M. K. D. Cann, p. 248. Arnold Shankman, "A Jury of Her Peers: The South Carolina Woman and Her Campaign for Jury Service," *South Carolina Historical Magazine*, 81:102. South Carolina didn't ratify the Nineteenth Amendment until 1969.

117. Shankman, pp. 103–04.

118. Wallace, 3:478.

119. Lofton, pp. 1–2. Barton, pp. 120–25.

120. Fields, pp. 223–24. M. K. D. Cann, p. 36.

121. Hayes, p. 406. M. K. D. Cann, p. 19.

122. John G. Sproat and Larry Schweikart, *Making Change: South Carolina Banking in the Twentieth Century* (Columbia, 1990), p. 85. Hayes, p. 5.

123. Robertson, p. 282.

124. Hayes, pp. 528–29.

125. Hayes, pp. 218–21.

126. Lofton, pp. 151–54. Hayes, p. 6.

127. Hayes, pp. 6, 173. Jones, *South Carolina*, p. 639. Lofton, pp. 5, 32, 60, 71.

128. Fields, pp. 223–24.

129. Hayes, pp. 173–75, 184–99. State government had done little to help the situation. In 1931 Governor John G. Richards had vetoed the appropriation for the State Board of Public Welfare after his attempts to abolish the agency had failed. M. K. D. Cann, 232.

130. Hayes, p. 188.

131. Hayes, pp. 264–69. Jones, *South Carolina*, pp. 641–42, 647. Some 23.2 percent of the population was on relief. Only Florida had a higher percentage. Because 60.2 percent of South Carolina's population was under twenty-five, the percentage of young people on relief was correspondingly higher. Hayes, pp. 176–77.

132. Hayes, pp. 248, 260–62. Lofton, pp. 149–50.

133. Edgar, *Santee Cooper*, pp. 6–11.

134. Hayes, pp. 411–19. Edgar, ed., *South Carolina*, p. 65.

135. Hayes, pp. 406, 454.

136. Hayes, pp. 523–24.

137. Jones, *Synoptic History*, p. 265.

138. Jones, *Synoptic History*, p. 264.

139. Carlton, "Unbalanced Growth," pp. 121–24.

140. Jones, *South Carolina*, p. 650.

141. Hollis, "'Cotton Ed Smith'—Showman or Statesman?," *South Carolina Historical Magazine*, 71:235, 242.

142. Hollis, "Cotton Ed," pp. 249–51.

143. Hollis, "Cotton Ed," pp. 248–49. "'Palmetto Stump'—Thirties Style," *Time*, 28 (24 August 1936), reprinted in Lander and Ackerman, pp. 349–53.

144. Marvin L. Cann, "The End of Political Myth: The South Carolina Gubernatorial Campaign of 1838." *South Carolina Historical Magazine*, 72:139, 142–49.

145. Hayes, pp. 275–76. Jones, *Synoptic History*, p. 249.

146. James F. Byrnes, *All in One Lifetime* (New York, 1958), pp. 59–66. Hayes, pp. 7, 10–26.

147. Hayes, p. 33.

148. Jones, *South Carolina*, p. 636.

149. Hayes, pp. 55–65.

150. Hayes, p. 465–67.

151. Byrnes, pp. 96–107. Hayes, pp. 150, 492.

152. Hollis, "Cotton Ed," p. 252.

153. Hayes, pp. 463, 505.

154. Lofton, pp. 248–49.

155. Hayes, pp. 506–08, 522.

156. Robertson, pp. 295–96. Robertson's epitaph (printed in the introduction to the 1960 edition) was a clear statement of his attachment to his beloved Carolina hills:

"I rest in thy bosom, Carolina.
Thy earth and thy air around and
above me. In my own country,
among my own, I sleep."

Chapter 3—Ignited By War, 1941–1966

1. South Carolina State Development Board, *South Carolina Servicemen After the War* (n.p., 1945), pp. 7–8, 14–15. Newby, p. 275.

2. Enid Ewing, "Charleston Contra Mundum," *Nation*, 157:579–81. Lander, p. 209.

3. Ewing, pp. 579–81.

4. Ewing, pp. 580–81.

5. Ewing, pp. 580–81.

6. South Carolina Department of Agriculture, *Report of the Department of Agriculture of South Carolina to the General Assembly, 1941–1942*, pp. 47, 150.

7. Lander, p. 210.

8. South Carolina Department of Labor, *Annual Report of the Department of Labor, 1941–1942*, pp. 18, 21–24; *1950–1951*, pp. 24–25.

9. *South Carolina Servicemen After the War*, pp. 7–9, 28.

10. *South Carolina Servicemen After the War*, p. 28.

11. South Carolina Department of Agriculture, *Report, 1945–1946*, p. 25.

12. *South Carolina Servicemen After the War*, pp. 30–31.

13. Albert D. Hutto to the editor of *The State*, 5 August 1944. Copy in Dr. Wil Lou Gray Papers, South Caroliniana Library.

14. "Killbillies," *Newsweek*, 1 May 1944, p. 33. V. O. Key, *Southern Politics in State and Nation* (New York, 1949), pp. 626–27. Lander, pp. 169–71.

15. Key, p. 628. Samuel Grafton, "Lonesomest Man in Town," *Collier's*, 29 April 1950, p. 50.

16. Lander, p. 171.

17. Rebecca West, "Opera in Greenville," in Lander and Ackerman, pp. 361–69. "Lynch Trial Makes Southern History," *Life*, 2 June 1947, pp. 27–31.

18. Files of *The State*, "Industry: General (W. D. Workman, 1945–1956, 1956–1961)," 28 August 1947, 19 December 1945.

19. Files of *The State*, "Industry: General (Workman)," *Record* (Columbia), 19 December 1945.

20. Files of *The State*, "Industry: General (Workman)," 19 December 1945, 23 April 1946, 28 August 1947.

21. Files of *The State*, "Industry: General (Workman)," 19 December 1945.

22. Ann D. Edwards, George D. Terry, Walter B. Edgar, George C. Rogers, Jr., and Augustus T. Graydon, *The Governor's Mansion of the Palmetto State* (Columbia, 1978), p. 71. Byrnes, p. 411. Files of *The State*, "Industry: General (Workman)," 30 August 1947.

23. Files of *The State*, "Industry: General (Workman)," 2 August 1947.

24. Files of *The State*, "Industry: General (Workman)," 9 January 1957.

25. Files of *The State*, "Industry: General (Workman)," 28 August 1947.

26. Byrnes, p. 411.

27. James C. Cobb, *The Selling of the South: The Southern Crusade for Industrial Development, 1936–1980* (Baton Rouge, 1982), p. 230. Files of *The State*, "Industry: General (Workman)," from the *News and Courier* (Charleston), 14 May 1958 and "Industry: South Carolina Development Board (1955–1983)," 22 January 1967.

28. Files of *The State*, " Industry: General (Workman)," 24 August 1955.

29. Files of *The State*, "Textiles: General (1955–1983)," 3 July 1955, 10 July 1955, 11 September 1955, 23 November 1955.

30. The act was named for representatives James Morris Arthur and John Calhoun Hart of Union County. Files of *The State*, "Textiles," 15 March 1956. Edgar, ed., *The Biographical Directory of the South Carolina House of Representatives, Volume I: Session Lists, 1692–1973* (Columbia, 1974), p. 589.

31. Files of *The State*, "Textiles," 27 March 1956, 3 April 1956, 24 June 1956.

32. Files of *The State*, "Textiles," 30 March 1956; 5, 6, 7, 17 April 1956; 2 May 1956; 28 September 1956.

33. Files of *The State*, "Textiles," 28, 29 September 1956.

34. South Carolina State Development Board, *South Carolina News*, September 1962.

35. South Carolina State Ports Authority, *Port News*, December 1951, p. 7; November 1955, p. 11; December 1959, pp. 3, 7; January 1960, pp. 8–9. South Carolina State Development Board, *Annual Report, 1948–1949*, p. 25. *South Carolina on the March: 1943–1958, Fifteen Years of Progress*, p. 31.

36. South Carolina State Ports Authority, *Port News*, December 1959, p. 7.

37. South Carolina State Development Board, *South Carolina News*, September 1962.

38. Files of *The State*, "Industry: General (Workman)," 17 May 1959.

39. Cobb, *The Selling of the South*, p. 166.

40. Cobb, *The Selling of the South*, pp. 167, 169. South Carolina State Development Board, "Technical Training in South Carolina" (n.p., 1968?), pp. 4–5, 8–9. Cobb, *Industrialization and Southern Society, 1877–1984* (Lexington, KY, 1984), p. 106.

41. Files of *The State*, "Industry: SC Development Board," 6 March 1957. South Carolina State Development Board, *Fifteen Years*, pp. 5, 16.

42. South Carolina State Development Board, *South Carolina News*, July 1960. *State Magazine*, 16 January 1949, p. 13.

43. South Carolina Department of Agriculture, *Report, 1959–1960,* p. 140.

44. Petty, *Twentieth Century,* pp. 20–21.

45. Gavin Wright, *Old South, New South: Revolution in the Southern Economy Since the Civil War* (New York, 1986), fig. 8.2, pp. 245–46. Newby, p. 295.

46. South Carolina Department of Agriculture, *Report, 1955–1956,* p. 55. Lander, p. 225.

47. Barton, pp. 271–74.

48. Testifying before a committee of the General Assembly, Dean Samuel L. Prince of the University of South Carolina's Law School was asked why it was so expensive to establish and maintain a new law school at South Carolina State College. He said: "Gentlemen, well I'll tell you. The price of prejudice is very high." Augustus T. Graydon, a Columbia attorney, was present and witnessed the exchange. Interview with Augustus T. Graydon, 10 July 1991.

49. Fields, pp. 55, 72–73. M. K. D. Cann, pp. 269.

50. Howard H. Quint, *Profile in Black and White: A Frank Portrait of South Carolina* (Washington, 1958), pp. 11, 102. Newby, p. 351.

51. South Carolina didn't do that well with whites, either; in 1948, some 18 percent were illiterate. Newby, p. 308.

52. Quint, pp. 12–13.

53. Byrnes, p. 407.

54. Byrnes, p. 408. Quint, pp. 15–16, 93.

55. *South Carolina's Educational Revolution* (n.p., n.d.). Byrnes, p. 408.

56. Byrnes, p. 408.

57. Byrnes, p. 408.

58. Byrnes, p. 418.

59. Quint, pp. 25–27.

60. Quint, pp. 38–42.

61. Julian Scheer, "The White Folks Fight Back," *New Republic,* 31 October 1955, pp. 9–12. Newby, p. 320. Quint, pp. 32, 48–49, 51–53, 56–57.

62. Lander, p. 202.

63. Scheer, pp. 10, 12. Quint, p. 98.

64. Quint, p. 99.

65. Lander, p. 203. Quint, p. 111.

66. Quint, pp. 178–79.

67. Quint, pp. 175–77.

68. Quint, pp. 116–23.

69. Review of Ernest M. Lander, Jr., *A History of South Carolina, 1865–1960* (Columbia, 1960), in the *News and Courier,* 25 September 1960, p. 11-C.

70. Charles Joyner, *Folk Song in South Carolina* (Columbia, 1971), pp. 107–08. Guy Carawon and Candie Carawon, recorders and editors, *Ain't you got a right to the Tree of Life? The People of Johns Island, South Carolina—Their Faces, Their Words, and Their Songs* (Athens, GA, revised and expanded edition, 1989), pp. 195, 208.

71. George McMillan, "Integration With Dignity," in Lander and Ackerman, p. 383.

72. McMillan, pp. 383–84.

73. McMillan, p. 385.

74. McMillan, pp. 388–89.

75. McMillan, p. 386.

76. McMillan, pp. 388–91.

77. Jack Bass and Walter DeVries, *The Transformation of Southern Politics: Social Change and Political Consequences Since 1945* (New York, 1976), p. 258. McMillan, p. 389.

78. McMillan, p. 390.

79. Paul S. Lofton, Jr., "Calm and Exemplary: Desegregation in Columbia, South Carolina," in Elizabeth Jacoway and David R. Colburn, *Southern Businessmen and Desegregation* (Baton Rouge 1982), pp. 70–81.

80. Cobb, *Industrialization and Southern Society,* p. 86.

81. "The South: Into a New Century," *Newsweek,* 3 May 1965, p. 27.

82. Newby, pp. 279, 326, 343–45. Lofton, "Calm and Exemplary," p. 81.

83. Inez Watson, editor, *Legislative Manual, 1960,* p. 265; *1966,* p. 272.

84. L. Ethan Ellis, *Steps in a Journey Toward Understanding: Activities of the New Jersey Civil War Centennial Commission in 1961* (Trenton, 1963), pp. 11–25.

85. South Carolina Confederate War Centennial Commission, *South Carolina Commemorates the Confederate*

War Centennial (n.p., n.d.). Supplement to Confederate Monuments and Markers in South Carolina, a manuscript in the Confederate Relic Room, Columbia, SC.

86. "The South: Into a New Century," p. 32.

87. John E. Huss, *Senator for the South: A Biography of Olin D. Johnston* (Garden City, NJ, 1961), p. 82.

88. Alberta Lachicotte, *Rebel Senator: Strom Thurmond of South Carolina* (New York, 1966), p. 106.

89. John C. Topping, Jr., John R. Lazarek, and William H. Linder, *Southern Republicanism and the New South* (Cambridge, MA, 1966), p. 92.

90. "The South: Into a New Century," p. 27.

91. South Carolina Budget Commission, *The South Carolina State Budget for the Fiscal Year Ending June 30, 1941*, p. 79; *1942*, pp. 29–30, 179–81, 357.

92. South Carolina State Budget and Control Board, *The South Carolina State Budget for the Fiscal Year Ending June 30, 1954*, p. 3; *1968*, pp. 29–30.

93. Key, pp. 152–53, 155.

94. William D. Workman, Jr., "The Ring That Isn't," in Lander and Ackerman, pp. 393, 398. Lander, pp. 185, 198.

CHAPTER 4—SOUTH CAROLINA, 1966–1991

1. Charles F. Kovacik and John J. Winberry, *South Carolina: A Geography* (Boulder, 1987), pp. 133–34. South Carolina State Budget and Control Board, *Economic Report, The State of South Carolina, 1972*: 51.

2. George C. Rogers, Jr., "Who Is a South Carolinian?," *South Carolina Historical Magazine*, 89:11–12.

3. Kovacik and Winberry, p. 149.

4. Kovacik and Winberry, p. 145. Jones, *South Carolina*, p. 686.

5. Kovacik and Winberry, p. 150.

6. *Economic Report, 1972*, 92–94. Kovacik and Winberry, pp. 159–60, 166.

7. Kovacik and Winberry, p. 162.

8. *Report of the Department of Agriculture, 1970–1971*, 3, 11, 30.

9. Charles B. Tyer, "The Special Purpose District in South Carolina," in Charles B. Tyer and Cole Blease Graham, Jr., eds., *Local Government in South Carolina, Volume I: The Governmental Landscape* (Columbia, 1984), pp. 82–83, 87.

10. "South Carolina Still Stinging Year Later," *Charlotte Observer*, 14 July 1991, pp. 1, 10-A. Gil Thelen to the author, 19 September 1990.

11. *Economist*, 18 August 1990, p. 21. *Economist*, 13 April 1991, cited in *The State*, 14 May 1991, p. 8-A.

12. Probably the best of the reports was "Scandals Cloud Life in South Carolina," *New York Times*, 12 May 1991, p. 11.

13. Interview with Charles W. Coolidge of Columbia, 5 June 1991.

14. *The State*, 26 August 1990, p. 2-D. Beginning with a series of special investigative and editorial reports entitled "Power Failure," *The State* has taken a hard look at the very nature of South Carolina government. The three branches of government and various state agencies all have come under close scrutiny. *The State*, 5, 12, 19, 26 May 1991; 17, 23 June 1991; 7 July 1991; 11 August 1991; 1, 22 September 1991; 13, 20 October 1991; 24 November 1991; 15 December 1991.

15. *The State*, 23 February 1991, p. 3-B.

16. Since 1920, there have been twelve studies of South Carolina state government. All called for some sort of reform or restructuring. All referred to lack of accountability, fragmentation, and inefficiency: the same problems vexing the state in 1991. South Carolina State Reorganization Commission, *On Reorganization: An Overview of Theory, Practice, and the South Carolina Experience* (Columbia, 1991), p. 35.

17. Bass and DeVries, p. 260.

18. Jack W. Germond and John Witcover, "GOP Gains as Blacks Seek High Office," *The State*, 29 May 1990, p. 6-A. *Black Elected Officials: A National Roster* (Washington, 1989), p. 375.

19. Bass and DeVries, p. 263.

20. Jones, *South Carolina*, p. 668.

21. Jones, *South Carolina*, pp. 664–65.

22. Newby, p. 331. Jones, *South Carolina*, pp. 664–65.

23. *The State*, 9, 18 February 1970; *Greenville News*, 23 January 1970, Scrapbooks, The Robert Evander McNair Papers, Institute for Southern Studies, University of South Carolina, Columbia, SC.

24. Neal R. Pierce, *The Deep South States of America: People, Politics, and Power in the Seven Deep South States* (New York, 1974), pp. 395–96. *Piedmont* (Greenville), 28 January 1970; *Greenville News*, 28 January 1970, Scrapbooks, McNair Papers.

25. *The State*, 12 February 1970, McNair Papers. Pierce, p. 396.

26. *Observer* (Charlotte), 9 March 1970, *Greenville News*, 18 March 1970, *The State*, 9, 21 February 1970, McNair Papers. Pierce, p. 396.

27. *News and Courier* (Charleston), 27 June 1970, McNair Papers.

28. "All Desegregation Orders Obeyed—Then School Chaos in Greenville, S.C.," *US News and World Report*, 7 December 1970: 26–28.

29. Eleanor Poats, *Spartanburg County School District Seven: The First Ninety-Eight Years, 1884–1982* (Spartanburg, 1982), p. 93.

30. South Carolina High School League, *Palmetto's Finest* (Columbia, 1989), pp. 48–52. South Carolina State Department of Education, *School Directory of South Carolina, 1955–56, 1969–1970, 1970–1971, 1988–1989.*

31. State Department of Education, *Annual Report, 1956*, p. 181.

32. Quint, pp. 63–64.

33. For a discussion of the desegregation of private schools in the South see Zebulon Vance Wilson, *They Took Their Stand: The Integration of Southern Private Schools* (Atlanta, 1983), passim.

34. Robert J. Steeley, "A History of Independent Education in South Carolina" (Ph.D. dissertation, University of South Carolina, 1979), pp. 91, 97, 111–12, passim. State Department of Education, *Annual Report, 1976–1977*, pp. 220, 241, 299.

35. Files of *The State*, "Schools: Private, General," 13 July 1986.

36. In January 1982, *The State* reported that twenty-three private schools either did not have or had lost their tax-exempt status because of discriminatory admissions policies. Files of *The State*, "Schools: Private, General," 22 January 1982.

37. Files of *The State*, "Schools: Private, General," 30 May 1983.

38. Interview with J. Robert Shirley of Columbia, 19 January 1990.

39. Moody's Investor Services, *Opportunity and Growth in South Carolina, 1968–1985* (New York, 1968), pp. 49, 53.

40. Interview with William R. McKinney, Jr., Governor Riley's press secretary, 8 March 1990.

41. South Carolina State Department of Education, *EIA V: A Report on the Education Improvement Act of 1984 and South Carolina's Continuing Quest for Quality Public School Education* (Columbia, 1989).

42. Interview with William R. McKinney, Jr., 19 February 1990.

43. Marshall Frady, *Southerners: A Journalist's Odyssey* (New York, 1980), p. 286.

44. Cobb, *The Selling of the South*, pp. 240–42. "The Showdown at Hilton Head," *Business Week*, 17 April 1971, p. 102. "Environment: Fight at Hilton Head," *Newsweek*, 13 April 1970, pp. 72–75.

45. Frady, p. 287.

46. Frady, p. 290.

47. "Fight at Hilton Head," *Newsweek*, 13 April 1970: 71–72.

48. Frady, p. 301.

49. Frady, pp. 289–90.

50. Cobb, *The Selling of the South*, pp. 248–50.

51. Files of *The State*, "GSX," *Record* (Columbia), 18 March 1986.

52. Interview with Dr. Winona B. Vernberg, dean of the School of Public Health, University of South Carolina, 15 May 1990.

53. The Housing and Urban Development Act of 1968 (and as amended in 1969 and 1972) now provided homeowners and developers with the opportunity to build expensive homes and resorts right on the beach. Prior to the federal flood insurance program, most South Carolina beach houses were modest cottages whose owners were willing to take a loss. In 1991 there are million-dollar "beach houses" in the manner of the Newport "cottages" of a century ago.

54. Robert L. Janiskee, "Storm of the Century: Hurricane Hugo and the Impact on South Carolina," *Southeastern Geographer*, 30 May 1990, p. 66.

55. A term used in the *Palmetto Leader*, a black Columbia newspaper. *Palmetto Leader*, 10 May 1930, p. 4.

56. Benjamin Mays, *Born to Rebel* (Brown Thrasher edition, Athens, 1987). Introduction by Vernon E. Burton, pp. ix–x, xlvii, 1, 37, 41, 49.

57. Emma Gelders Sterne, *Mary*

McLeod Bethune (New York, 1957), pp. 1–66. Rackham Holt, *Mary McLeod Bethune: A Biography* (Garden City, NY, 1964), pp. 1–32.

58. Miller, "These 'Colored' United States," pp. 377, 400.

59. Julia Boublitz Morgan, "Son of a Slave," *Johns Hopkins Magazine*, June 1981, pp. 20–26.

60. Miller, *Race Adjustment: Essays on the Negro in America* (New York, 1909), pp. 285–86.

61. Brawley, p. 309.

62. Thomas L. Johnson, "South Carolina Academy of Authors," *Carologue*, vol. 7, no. 1 (Spring 1991): 13. Among Brawley's works are *A Short History of the American Negro* (New York, 1913); *A Social History of the American Negro* (New York, 1921); *Negro Builders and Heroes* (Chapel Hill, 1937); and *The Negro in Literature and Culture* (New York, 1921).

63. *The Palmetto Leader*, 9 August 1930, p. 4.

64. *Columbia Record*, 13 March 1980, p. 8-E.

65. *New York Times*, 30 July 1972, section 10, p. 1. *Trends*, June 1971, p. 5.

66. *Film Comment*, 6 May 1973.

67. Deborah Solomon, "The Unflagging Artistry of Jasper Johns," *New York Times Magazine*, 19 June 1988, pp. 20–23.

68. "Jesse Jackson," undated newspaper clipping in vertical files, South Caroliniana Library.

69. *The State*, 13 March 1988, p. 1-A.

Suggested Readings

A great deal has been written about twentieth-century South Carolina, but not much of it has been printed in book form. Much of the material is scattered in popular and scholarly journals. References to these articles, to a wealth of primary sources, and to more specialized works can be found in the endnotes.

Among the best sources on the period are the dissertations written by graduate students. Of particular note are Mary Katharine Cann's "The Morning After: South Carolina in the Jazz Age," John Duffy's "Charleston Politics in the Progressive Era," Jack Irby Hayes, Jr.'s "South Carolina and the New Deal, 1932–1938," Theodore Hemingway's "Beneath the Yoke of Bondage: A History of Black Folks in South Carolina, 1900–1940," and Paul Lofton's "A Social and Economic History of Columbia, South Carolina During the Great Depression, 1929–1940." With the exception of Lofton, all were students at the University of South Carolina, and Lofton was a South Carolina native.

The list of suggested readings is by no means inclusive. Rather, it is meant to provide the reader with a ready reference for further study on a variety of topics.

Browning, Wilt. *Linthead: Growing Up in a Carolina Cotton Mill Village.* Asheboro, NC: Down Home Press, 1990.

Burts, Richard M. *Richard Irvine Manning and the Progressive Movement in South Carolina.* Columbia: University of South Carolina Press, 1974.

Byrnes, James F. *All in One Lifetime.* New York: Harper and Brothers, 1958.

Carlton, David L. *Mill and Town in South Carolina, 1880–1920.* Baton Rouge: Louisiana State University Press, 1982.

Clark, Septima P., with LeGette Blythe. *Echo in My Soul.* New York: E. P. Dutton, 1962.

Cobb, James C. *The Selling of the South: The Southern Crusade for Industrial Development, 1936–1980.* Baton Rouge: Louisiana State University Press, 1982.

Coclanis, Peter A. *The Shadow of a Dream: Economic Life and Death in the South Carolina Lowcountry, 1670–1920.* New York: Oxford University Press, 1989.

Cooper, William J., Jr. *The Conservative Regime: South Carolina, 1876–1890.* Baltimore: Johns Hopkins University Press, 1968.

Doyle, Don H. *New Men, New Cities, New South.* Chapel Hill: University of North Carolina Press, 1990.

Edgar, Walter B., ed. *South Carolina: The WPA Guide to the Palmetto State.* Columbia: University of South Carolina Press, 1988.

Fields, Mamie Garvin, with Karen Fields. *Lemon Swamp and Other Places: A South Carolina Memoir.* New York: Free Press, 1983.

Fox, William Price. *Moonshine Light, Moonshine Bright.* New York: Bantam Books, 1970.

Gordon, Asa B. *Sketches of Negro Life and History in South Carolina.* 2nd ed. Columbia: University of South Carolina Press, 1971.

Graham, Cole Blease, Jr., and Charles B. Tyer. *Local Government in South Carolina, Volume I: The Governmental Landscape; Volume II: Problems and Perspectives.* Columbia: Bureau of Governmental Research and Service, 1984.

Heyward, DuBose. *Mamba's Daughters.* New York: Literary Guild, 1929.

Hollis, Daniel W. *University of South Carolina Vol. II: From College to University.* Columbia: University of South Carolina Press, 1956.

Jones, Lewis P. *Books and Articles on South Carolina History.* 2nd ed. Columbia: University of South Carolina Press, 1991.

Jones, Lewis P. *Stormy Petrel: N. G. Gonzales and His State.* Columbia, 1973.

Kovacik, Charles F. and John J. Winberry. *South Carolina: A Geography.* Columbia: University of South Carolina Press, 1989.

Lander, Ernest M., Jr. *A History of South Carolina, 1865–1960.* Columbia: University of South Carolina Press, 1960.

Mays, Benjamin. *Born to Rebel.* Brown Thrasher, ed. Introduction by Vernon E. Burton. Athens, GA: University of Georgia Press, 1987.

Moore, John Hammond. *The South Carolina Highway Department, 1917–1987.* Columbia: University of South Carolina Press, 1987.

Newby, Idus A. *Black Carolinians: A History of Blacks in South Carolina from 1895 to 1968.* Columbia: University of South Carolina Press, 1973.

Peterkin, Julia. *Scarlet Sister Mary.* Indianapolis: Bobbs-Merrill, 1928.

Rice, John Andrew. *I Came Out of the Eighteenth Century.* New York: Harper and Brothers, 1942.

Robertson, Ben. *Red Hills and Cotton: An Upcountry Memory.* Introduction by Lacy K. Ford. Southern Classics Series edition. Columbia: University of South Carolina Press, 1991.

Simkins, Francis Butler. *Pitchfork Ben Tillman: South Carolinian.* Baton Rouge, 1944.

Sproat, John G. and Larry Schweikart. *Making Change: South Carolina Banking in the Twentieth Century.* Columbia: South Carolina Bankers Association, 1990.

Tindall, George B. *South Carolina Negroes, 1877–1900.* Columbia: University of South Carolina Press, 1952.

Woodward, C. Vann. *The Strange Career of Jim Crow.* 2nd. rev. ed. New York: Oxford University Press, 1966.

INDEX

World Columbian Exposition (Chicago), 143

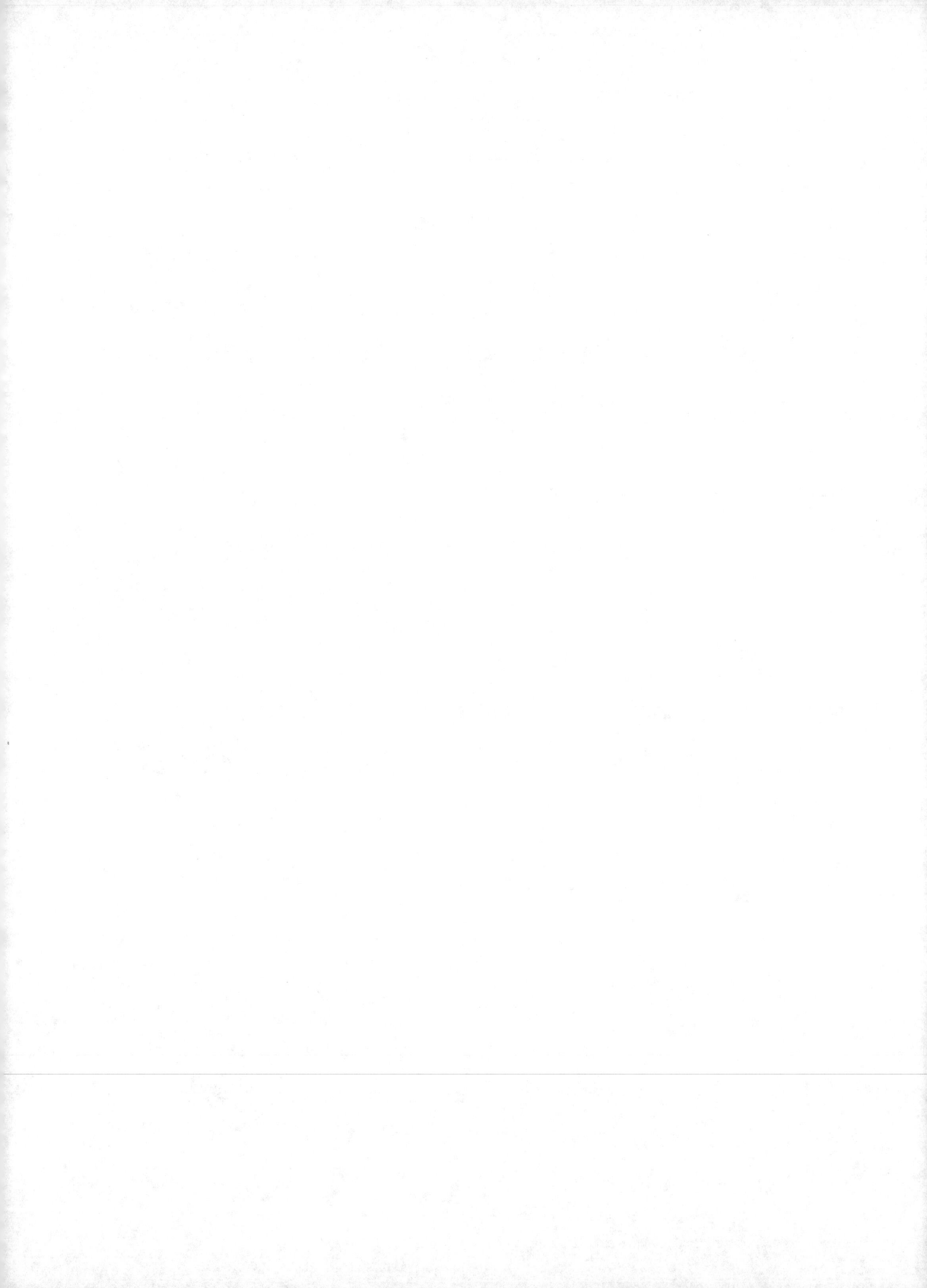